The Jackie Stewart Book of Shooting

The Jackie Stewart
Book of Shooting

with Mike Barnes

HarperCollins*Publishers*

First published in 1991
by HarperCollins Publishers,
77–85 Fulham Palace Road,
Hammersmith, London W6 8JB

9 8 7 6 5 4 3 2 1

British Library Cataloguing in Publication Data

Stewart, Jackie
The Jackie Stewart Book of Shooting
1. Shooting (Field sports)
I. Mike Barnes
799.313

ISBN 0 00 215587 7

Typeset in Itek Garamond by
Ace Filmsetting Ltd, Frome, Somerset

Printed and bound in Hong Kong

Contents

ACKNOWLEDGEMENTS

The authors would like to offer their warm appreciation to Bob Atkins, Glyn Morris, Gary Talbot and the *Shooting Gazette* for providing the photographic material for this book and Donald Green for his sketches, and to thank them for their kind permission to reproduce their material.

This book is dedicated to the three men who had a great deal to do with me developing as a man, as well as becoming an enthusiastic shot:

My father, who was a great inspiration to me – a wonderful angler and shot.

My grandfather, who was an example of elegance in gun-handling that I will never forget.

Glynne Jones, who taught me how to lose as well as win.

The Sport and its Appeal

Around the world clay pigeon shooting has become one of the fastest-growing participation sports, with some particularly significant developments in both Britain and the USA in recent years. It has been especially interesting for me over the last five years or so to notice the dramatic growth of interest in shooting.

For so long this was a sport which was perceived as the preserve of game shooters, predominantly wealthy landowners who had the exclusive rights to shoot on their vast tracts of land. Driven pheasant, partridge and grouse were the order of the day, and even after the break-up of many of the great estates, those who had neither the financial means for game shooting nor the necessary connections were mostly reluctant to settle for the option of shooting clay pigeons. 'He's a clay shooter' was the dismissive phrase which actually said as much about snobbery as anything else!

So what has changed? The image of clay pigeon shooting has altered dramatically. In my view this is largely due to well-known personalities being seen enjoying the sport both on television and at charity events attended by the public.

Because of my own involvement with the sport from an early age I was very aware of the challenge and pleasure to be had and because it opened so many doors for me early in my career I felt that on retirement from motor racing I would endeavour to repay my debt. As a consequence, the first of the Jackie Stewart Celebrity Challenge Shoots was held at the North Wales Shooting School, near Chester. We invited dukes, lords, royals, stars of the film and entertainment industries and famous names from the world of sport. With the help of sponsors such as Rolex, who have now sponsored the event for many years, we created a glamorous occasion. The television cameras came along and clay shooting claimed substantial exposure on the small screen. Since that time I am delighted to say that the Celebrity Challenges, which are now held at my shooting school at the Gleneagles Hotel in Perthshire, have become enormously popular events. We find that prominent people are keen to come and take part. And while they have a good time some also take the competition very seriously indeed.

Not only does it make for good television and raise a lot of money for charity, it has also brought the appeal of clay shooting into millions of homes around the world. I would not wish to claim that I have been solely responsible for the popularity of the sport, but these celebrity events, I feel, have undoubtedly had a considerable impact.

With the shooting school at Gleneagles we have also developed a ground with the kind of facilities which have for so long been lacking in the sport. From the time I left competitive clay shooting to my return at the end of my motor-racing days, thirteen years in all, little had changed. There was virtually nothing in terms of facilities at most of the grounds – little wonder that the same old faces were still dominating the circuit. New blood wasn't being attracted. That has changed very much now and new people are flocking to the sport and discovering its joys.

To give an idea of the number of newcomers, consider this: in five years our school at Gleneagles became the busiest shooting school in the world with some 12,500 people shooting on our range per annum; and yet 60 per cent of the customers had never held a gun before. And 40 per cent were women. This number of women taking up the sport is an interesting factor, and our instructors find that they make extremely good pupils.

All newcomers quickly discover the real pleasure of clay

shooting. While our Celebrity Challenges are great fun and enjoyable to watch because of the people taking part, generally speaking this is not a spectator sport. But as a participation sport it has few equals. I can think of no other in which a pupil can within one hour's tuition achieve a 50 per cent success rate. There is immense gratification with each successful shot – and that satisfaction is also visible and immediate. Each broken clay brings a rewarding experience to the person who is pulling the trigger.

You only have to see the look on people's faces to know that they are enjoying the experience. Many of the people I have invited to the Challenge have become hooked on the sport and in the process turned into very capable shots. From the world of motor racing Martin Brundle, Nigel Mansell, Derek Bell and Jonathan Palmer are all excellent shots, as are top jockeys Steve Cauthen and Willie Carson. Actor Anthony Andrews and film director Steven Spielberg are now very keen shots. Top British Olympic javelin thrower Tessa Sanderson showed great skill while Kiri Te Kanawa is another who has become a very good shot.

Not only is it a great sport for newcomers, it also has much to offer in terms of sporting and individual challenge with clay shooting disciplines and targets to test the ability of the very best. It is both a fun sport and a competitive challenge at every level from local charity events to national and international championships and, the ultimate test, the Olympic Games. Both trap and skeet are Olympic sports.

The number of game shots also taking to clay pigeons is far greater than ever before. Lord Lichfield, who has his own very attractive shooting ground in Staffordshire, is one of many fine game shots who take advantage of clays for further enjoyment out of season.

Like anything in life, practice makes perfect. Becoming a good shot is not something that happens spontaneously. And while there are certain individuals who have exceptional hand–eye co-ordination, it is a gift which they still

need to develop for good consistent shooting just like anyone else.

Shooting is like motor racing in this respect. It is one
thing being a good driver but winning a race, let alone a
championship, tests all the skills and character of the competitor. It often puzzles me that so many game shots go out
at the start of the season expecting to pick up from where
they left off some nine months earlier. The only way to
become a really good consistent shot is to work at it.

In any other sport, practice is accepted as a natural and
important part of it all. Sportsmen and women at the peak
of their professions devote a tremendous amount of time
to practice. Nick Faldo or Greg Norman, for instance, can
go out and hit 300 balls in order to improve their swing or
correct a hook or slice. That amount of repetition and
learning experience inevitably brings its rewards. Ivan
Lendl similarly might spend five hours in which he will
serve virtually continually in an attempt to perfect a certain aspect of his service. Even those with that wonderful
gift of natural talent cannot perform to their best without
much practice and coaching. It is readily accepted that all
top sportsmen look for coaching to improve performance
from time to time.

Yet for some reason many game shots never even consider the possibility. In my opinion it simply isn't possible
to become a consistent game shot without practice and to
that end it is pure folly to pick up a gun on the first outing
of a new season with the expectation of bringing down the
highest and fastest birds with any consistency. That applies
even to such excellent shots as the Duke of Roxburghe and
Lord Stafford, who enjoy the privilege of many invitations.
To shoot consistently from the outset, all shooters should
previously have spent time in practice.

Clay pigeon shooting presents the perfect opportunity
of out-of-season practice. Some say that the targets are different and nothing like the real thing – that depends on
how the targets are presented – but even at their worst,

they still serve to remind the shooter just how crucial it is to stand and mount the gun correctly, and that without the accompanying smooth swing the shot and target will continue to elude one another. More and more people are now recognizing this. As the facilities at many grounds improve, these people are also finding that the practice is hugely enjoyable in its own right. A number of grounds also offer summer season tickets which are excellent value.

The other big new area of clay pigeon shooting activity is that of corporate entertainment. Going back only a few years there were just one or two people offering such a facility. My colleagues and close friends Allan and Noel Jones at the North Wales Shooting School were among the first to present the idea to companies in the Chester, Manchester and Liverpool area.

The West London Shooting Grounds and Holland & Holland Shooting School both saw the opportunities early on and for some time have found favour with many major companies who see clay shooting as an ideal option for corporate entertainment. Down in Cheltenham, Christopher Coley, with great initiative, set up a scheme offering companies and their clients the opportunity of shooting clays in the grounds of stately homes. The scheme proved a great success. Shadowbrook are very mobile and arrange shooting in many varied locations.

Similarly once we opened the school at Gleneagles we attracted a lot of business from the world of commerce. It provides a genuinely alternative day out for companies looking to indulge their customers. In our own instance, the company can offer clients a superb time in the grounds of a fabulous five-star hotel. They are kitted out from head to toe in all the correct clothing, with a full range of Barbour weatherwear and Hunter wellingtons, as appropriate to the conditions. We have a lovely shooting lodge and an excellent team of instructors. Having been to all of the usual golf, tennis and racing days, they find clay shooting is like a breath of fresh air. Physique does not come into it – nor does age, sex or even previous experience.

While it is difficult to enjoy a game of golf on the very first outing, anyone under the supervision of a skilled instructor can enjoy a degree of proficiency at clays. Consequently they can derive enormous pleasure from their sense of achievement in such a short time. At Gleneagles all the pleasures of being a spectator are there with fine food, service, setting and good company, plus the added thrill of successful participation. It is a very potent combination and is now being used extensively.

So, there is the game shooter who practises on clays more readily than ever before, there is the booming industry of clay shooting as a means of corporate entertainment and, of course, clay pigeon shooting as a sport in its own right.

Clay shooting, either competitive or informal, now has an enormous following, attracting people from all walks of life. When I first shot competitively as a young teenager, trap (or 'Down-the-Line') was the most popular form. Fairly straightforward going-away targets which nevertheless demand great powers of concentration to produce a winning score. Nowadays it is Sporting which accounts for a considerable majority of the sport's participants. Sporting clay shooting has evolved from game shooting practice. In effect it is the simulation of quarry species, with clay targets presented to the shooter to represent a driven pheasant, crossing pigeon, springing teal and any number of other variations.

Such targets can be presented with varying degrees of difficulty according to the type of shooter. A novice can enjoy a nice simple fairly slow-driven bird, while an experienced sporting shot will be looking for something very much more challenging. Often natural settings are used, thus enhancing the overall feel of the sport. Traps are concealed behind trees, hedgerows, or in dips so as to contrive a realistic situation. Apart from being a natural development of clay pigeon shooting, it also has the advantage of giving clubs of all sizes the opportunity of laying on good shoots without installing permanent facilities. Similarly for those who have perhaps neither the wish nor the time to travel to take part in big competitions, they can go along to their local club or shooting ground and be offered a different challenge on each occasion.

There is, therefore, the degree of unpredictability in this discipline, and as a consequence each course or layout can be shot purely for the pleasure of the personal challenge.

Trap shooting meanwhile also presents a personal challenge but in a different sense. While sporting is probably more of a test of shooting skill, trap is very much about competition and mental approach. Trap shooting is a test of nerve – one momentary lapse in concentration and a competition is lost – unlike sporting, where lost ground on one particular stand may be regained on another stand (what may be an awkward target for one competitor may be to the liking of another).

Skeet is the shooting of targets from two trap houses set 40 yards apart. There are seven shooting positions (or stations) formed in a semi-circle, so that during a round of 25 each competitor will shoot a variety of targets as they are thrown on fixed trajectories from the two traps. As such, it is good general practice for gun mount and swing. Again as the targets on each round of 25 will be the same on every layout, it is possible to master skeet to near perfection, from which point it comes down to concentration and having the mental approach which will give you the winning edge. I will deal with trap and skeet in more detail in Chapter 6.

Suffice to say, it is none too surprising that clay shooting is continuing to hit new heights of popularity. The sport's official body in Britain, the Clay Pigeon Shooting Association, has in the region of 28,000 members – this figure represents principally the more serious shooters, those who wish to take part in registered competitions. Consequently, its membership total is the tip of the proverbial iceberg, for the vast majority shoot exclusively on a local basis.

It is a sport which can be enjoyed equally by the old and the young, the tall and the short, both men and women, and cuts right across all social classes. It knows no boundaries. Its arrival in a major way is unquestionably down to one thing – its recognition as truly a sport for all.

The Rolex Jackie Stewart Celebrity Challenge was held biannually from 1982 to 1990 for charity, but its worldwide television coverage did much to raise the profile of the sport.

Some of the best amateur shots in the world competed in teams in the event: The Lords (*above, right*) – Stafford, Lichfield, Montagu and Romsey; The Dukes (*middle, right*) – Arion, Roxburghe, Abercorn and Atholl; The Ladies (*below, right*) – Marchioness of Ardales, Duchess of Roxburghe, Lady Fairhaven and Marchioness of Northampton

Rosemary, Marchioness of
Northampton

We made the event fun and entertaining,
but primarily it was a sporting spectacle,
and although the atmosphere was
friendly and jovial away from the range,
the competition between the top teams
in the traps was intense

Duke of Abercorn   Lord Lichfield

The Celebrity Challenge became quite a social event too, with some top entertainers providing glitter, and others adding further expertise to the field of competitors: Steven Spielberg (*left*) and Sean Connery are very keen shots, and Harrison Ford gave a fine performance for the Stars team; Selina Scott and Michael Parkinson (*above*) of the Broadcasters team talking tactics; Michael Winner (*below*), with Jenny Seagrove and Dame Tiri Te Kanawa, agreed that he's had far more successful shooting days – behind a camera!

...d by their captain the Duke of Kent (*above, far left*), ...e Team shot outstandingly well on the day; HRH Prince ...ward with Team-mates the King of the Hellenes (*above, ...ht*), and Sir Angus Ogilvy (*below*); Prince Edward on the ...ge (*inset*)

Imran Khan

Tracy Edwards in the pheasant trap

Clay shooting is one of the few sports where men and women can compete equally because strength is a far less significant factor than hand–eye coordination. In fact, the female shooters were some of the best competitors on the day

Anthony Andrews

Kenny Dalglish had an excellent day
shooting for the Sports Stars team

Selina Scott

The final group photograph and prize-giving – ever had one of those days when you've got to do everything yourself!

Michael Winner (*below*) and his team of entertainers had us laughing all day, but unfortunately they ended up with the Wooden Duck; Miss Marjorie Walker (*left*) presenting the magnificent Walkers Shortbread Trophy to the competition winners, The Lords.

But the real winners were the charities for whom w raised £200,000 on the day

1 Clay Pigeon Shooting Today

The basic 12-bore shotgun as we know it today has evolved over a period of 500 years. Guns have been used since the fourteenth century for firing on small animals and birds on the ground or water. There was little development until the mid seventeenth century when visitors to France returned home to tell friends that flintlocks were being used for 'shooting flying'. And from here there were the changes that took us from the muzzle loader to today's much more sophisticated weapon.

The tide of change began to gather momentum at the end of the eighteenth century when changes at the breech end of the 40-inch barrels were followed by the introduction of granulated gunpowder. This enabled the shortening of the barrels to take place reducing them to 32 inches and in turn led to the acceptance of the double-barrel shotgun. There were critics – there always are – but the changes were definitely for the better.

Then a truly significant change took place in 1807 when the Rev. A. J. Forsyth of Aberdeenshire in Scotland obtained a master patent on the use of a class of chemicals that exploded when struck to ignite, by percussion, the propelling charge. This really was a breakthrough as the sportsman now had a much more reliable gun in his hands and was no longer hampered by the damp disabling his flintlock.

This discovery ultimately led to the invention of the self-contained cartridge. Percussion ignition was initially applied to muzzle loaders, guns that still demanded a rather protracted reloading procedure, but through this technology the cartridge was just around the corner. It was essentially a French invention and its story starts with a Swiss ex-artillery man of Napoleon's day called Samuel Johannes Pauly who realized the potential that percussion ignition offered. In 1812 he obtained patent protection in France for a breech-loading gun and the cartridges for it. Though somewhat unsophisticated in design, this was the breakthrough which the sportsman needed and by the middle of the nineteenth century the cartridge had evolved into two practical forms – pinfire and centre fire.

Like anything new the breech-loading shotgun was initially met with much resistance. But gunmakers could see the enormous potential and a flush of patents followed. Gunmaking was a highly competitive business and the advent of the breech loader coincided with the emergence of driven game shooting in the UK.

Shooting had become a fashionable pastime in society from the mid nineteenth century. The hammerless gun was largely perfected by 1870; the 1880s saw the addition of the ejector mechanism, followed ten years later by the single-trigger mechanism. Much of this development took place in the UK where London gunmakers were vying for the lucrative business to be had amongst the pheasant- and grouse-shooting aristocracy. The extent of their shooting was legend.

It was a hugely innovative period, but strangely enough the English gun trade then took a back seat, notably to American John Moses Browning. Having met with little success in attempting to persuade gun manufacturers in his home country to look at his ideas, he took himself off to Belgium where he was met with open arms by FN (Fabrique National) at Liège. He gave us the classic five-shot semi-automatic shotgun, 9mm pistol and the gun that probably changed the course of gunmaking history, the B25 over-under. Just as Anson & Deeley had perfected the boxlock side-by-side, and the likes of Purdey had taken the sidelock side-by-side to the pinnacle of its design, so John Moses Browning blazed a new trail of his own with the B25. Patented in 1925, in production in 1926, the B25 is still going strong today relatively unchanged. Beretta's sidelock over-under, the SO, followed in 1932 and it too is still in production (indeed, this is the gun I now use).

The over-under is now universally accepted as the ideal gun for clay pigeon shooting (indeed I feel it's the best for all shooting), though the semi-automatic, of which the makers Remington and Beretta are market leaders, is hugely popular in America for both clays and game. The automatic is also much liked in Europe by the rough shooter (the walked-up game shooter).

The majority of today's gun production is in fact over-under and automatic. The side-by-side accounts for relatively few sales. Though still very popular for game shooting in the UK, and handed down from father to son, this barrel configuration will be of little use to the competitive shooter – over-unders and automatics are designed to win competitions.

Clay Target Shooting

From the invention of the first firearms in the fourteenth century through the next 400 years, weapons were used for two reasons – to gather food and for armed combat, both as efficiently as possible.

Professional hunters wanted to maximize every outing – being sportsmen did not come into it and the thought of shooting moving targets would probably have seemed ridiculous. In fairness, until the advent of the pinfire cartridge in the first half of the nineteenth century this was understandable. Loading a matchlock, wheel-lock or flint-lock gun was a lengthy process. The guns were heavy and in damp conditions owners could never be sure that they would fire. So they simply made the most of every shot.

This all changed, of course, with the development of breech-loading shotguns and self-contained cartridges in the middle of the nineteenth century. However, since time began man has always been keen to show off and compete. Spear throwing and sling contests were the equivalent of today's javelin and clay shooting competitions. And the competitive side of man's nature didn't wait for the breech-loading shotgun to pit his ability one against another's. I may be accused of bias, but it is fact that one of the first well-known shooting competitions was held in Scotland and known as the Popinjay. If I can quote from Chapter II of Sir Walter Scott's *Old Mortality*:

> The sheriff of the county of Lanark was holding the wappen-schaw of a wild district called the Upper Ward of Clydesdale, on a haugh or level plain, near to a royal borough, the name of which is no way essential to my story, on the morning of the 5th of May, 1679, when our narrative commences. When the musters had been made, and duly reported, the young men, as was usual, were to mix in various sports, of which the chief was to shoot at the popinjay or parrot. It was suspended to a pole, and served for a mark, at which the competitors discharged their fusees and carabines in rotation, at the distance of 60 or 70 paces. He whose ball brought down the mark, held the proud title of Captain of the Popinjay for the remainder of the day, and was usually escorted in triumph to the most reputable change-house in the neighbourhood, where the evening was closed with conviviality, conducted under his auspices, and, if he was able to sustain it, at his expense.

Just in case you were wondering – a popinjay was a stuffed effigy of a parrot!

Within approximately 50 years of that date the first trap shooting competition is thought to have taken place in

England. The targets were live pigeons and the first known shooting club was probably Hornsey Wood House Club, opened in 1810. From the outset this type of shooting was very much the preserve of the wealthy. Shoot meetings were great social occasions – the club at Notting Hill was superbly appointed with bar and dining room. A variety of traps was used to contain the birds before releasing them in front of the competitors. One of the most peculiar forms of shooting was the High Hat – a shooter placed a pigeon under a top hat at his feet and the object of the game was for the shooter to place the hat on his head before taking a shot at the retreating pigeon. Numerous trap clubs had been formed in England by 1850 and the sport had also by this time taken a foothold in America.

For a number of reasons the long-term potential of live pigeon shooting was always going to be limited. The fact that it was not an equal contest, and could depend upon luck, or worse, 'doctored birds', was just one worry. The other was the major criticism from groups who considered the sport to be barbaric. By the turn of the century, however, live pigeon shooting offered big purses at venues around the world. Some of the most prestigious competitions were held in Monte Carlo. In addition to big prize money live pigeon shooting has always been closely associated with gambling. As far back as 1869 Captain Adam Bogardus not only shot the first recorded 100 straight live pigeons at St Louis, he also won himself $2000 by shooting 500 pigeons in 528 minutes at another event in the same year.

The sport was banned in Britain in 1921, but still continues today in some countries around the world.

It was apparent to most, however, back in the 1860s, that live pigeons would inevitably run into problems. And the name Bogardus next crops up with a string of extraordinary feats at glass ball shooting. He had also become the major manufacturer of glass ball traps in the USA and his own performances couldn't have done business any harm! These targets were the invention of Charles Portlock of Boston, Massachusetts, who was inspired by the Japanese glass balls used on their fishing nets. Bogardus and Doc Carver were the American stars of the sport at the time and in 1879 Bogardus broke 5000 glass balls in 500 minutes, then went one better and shot 6000 in two consecutive days, breaking the first 3000 without a miss!

Shooting became a crowd-pulling turn also in the Wild West shows of the time where of course Annie Oakley made a name for herself. Annie was an exceptional shot and a real crowd pleaser – in 1885 at the end of the glass ball era she recorded what was probably her finest performance in shooting 4772 out of 5000 targets.

From Portlock's invention the 2½-inch glass ball target went through various throes of development. Launched into the air from a spring-loaded trap, they were soon embellished with feathers glued to the surface, then taken one step further by being loaded with feathers. This of course gave an impressive effect on being hit.

The glass ball was an interesting idea and certainly spectacular to watch, but had insurmountable shortcomings. It was difficult to make a consistent texture that could be transported safely yet break when hit with a pattern of pellets. But most importantly it was terribly messy. Glass ball ranges were covered in fragments and splinters which were terribly difficult to remove without ground staff cutting their hands.

But the target that was to change everything was now on the horizon. It is fascinating how America and the UK have continually made similar developments in the sport at around the same time as one another. In 1880 George Ligowsky of Cincinnati got the idea of a clay target from watching some boys skimming clam shells over the water of the Hudson river. He subsequently persuaded the boys to throw the shells in the air so that he could shoot at them. The shells were probably difficult to reproduce and obviously inconsistent in flight but they provided the inspiration for George to bake a clay target. At around the same time a man called McCaskey in England had the same idea and started making targets from pitch and river silt.

The first public exhibition of clay pigeon shooting took place at the end of the New York State Live Pigeon Shoot on Coney Island in 1880. By 1892 some 30 million clay targets had been used in America and the following year saw Britain's Inanimate Bird Association hold its first championship meeting at Wimbledon Park in July 1893. Traps were set at 18 yards rise and the format was based very much on live pigeon shooting. There were 44 competitors.

Clay pigeons were initially made entirely of clay and baked in brick ovens and were therefore extremely hard and difficult to break. A mixture of river silt and tar was then used, before moving on to chalk and pitch which remain the principal ingredients today.

Clay pigeon shooting was initially slow to catch on in a big way in Britain as the organizers were interested only in pitching the sport at those who already had lots of game shooting experience or were live pigeon enthusiasts. In America, however, this was not the case. The first National Championship was held in New Orleans in 1885 and was won by Doc Carver who shot straight, missing no targets, and who also that year shot 60,616 targets our of 64,000 in six days to establish an endurance record that has never been equalled. As mentioned, clay pigeons were added to the Grand American programme in 1900 and in 1903 this became a clays-only event. Martin Diefenderfer was the first champion with 94 out of 100.

Meanwhile back in Britain the first Dougall Memorial Trophy was shot for in 1896 and during the same year the first competition for women was held at Middlesex Gun Club which had its headquarters on the Westley Richards ground at the Welsh Harp, Hendon (the first in Europe, incidentally, with a trench for trappers). The now famous West London Shooting Grounds were opened in 1902 by Mr Richmond Watson and two years later the sport's governing body became the Clay Bird Shooting Association. It pleases me to note, however, that during the same year in Scotland Mr R. Campbell broke a British record, shooting 111 straight (using his second barrel only twice), which was the first recorded 100 straight in Britain.

Clays were shot in the 1906 'Interim' Olympic Games in Athens with the winner being an Englishman, Mr G. E. Merlin. How times change – the last Englishman to win the Olympic trap shooting event was Bob Braithwaite in 1968.

On both sides of the Atlantic clay shooting took a similar form – trap shooting with targets shot at 18 yards, later to be changed to 16 yards (as it is today), but a shot load of 1¼ ounces.

The 1914 British Championship attracted 2000 people for a full day's entertainment and music supplied by the Middlesex Regiment. Both clay and live bird shooting ceased in Britain in April 1916 and cartridges were controlled by the government. Permission to resume was given on 1 February 1919. In 1921, the year that live pigeon shooting was banned in Britain, the Perivale Gun Club was offering £50 as high gun prize – a lot of money at the time.

The twenties saw two other significant developments in the sport, however – skeet and sporting. The boom in driven pheasant shooting during Victorian and Edwardian times coincided with the introduction of the clay target. Game shooters were therefore able to practise on clays and London's leading shooting grounds were not slow to realize the potential offered by the new target. Simulated grouse, high towers for pheasant targets and other stands were created. Inevitably this evolved into a sport in its own right and 1925 saw the first British Sporting Championship at Albemarle Shooting Grounds, Worcester Park. Today this event is the biggest on the shooting calender, attracting 1500 entries. The competition was shot over two days, the first of which offered 10 walked-up, five pairs of grouse, 20 rocketing pheasants and 10 birds from the automatic trap. This was followed on the second day by 10 pairs of driven and five double rise. The automatic trap had been introduced to Britain in 1923.

Just as Britain invented sporting, skeet emerged from the United States. It arose as a result of a shooting game called 'around the clock', devised by the Davies family in Massachusetts in 1915. Shot fall-out on to neighbouring property forced them to reduce the shooting area to a semi-circle and the addition of an extra trap house (high house at 12 o'clock and low house at 6 o'clock). The game was popular in the area, and William Foster, a friend who helped devise the game, was assistant editor on the *National Sportsman* where in 1926 he wrote up a set of rules and published a competition to find a name for the game. The $100 prize attracted 10,000 entries with the winner being a lady from Montana called Gertrude Hurlbutt who suggested the Scandinavian word skeet (meaning 'shoot'). It was initially slow to catch on but the first tournament was held in 1935. Since that time of course it has become hugely popular all around the world.

There have been other developments over the years and various attempts have been made to introduce new disciplines. The rules of American trap are quite similar to those of English Down-the-Line, though neither is an Olympic discipline – at the Olympic Games it is possible to compete at Olympic trap and ISU skeet, the recognized international disciplines which are much more demanding than the regular forms of trap and skeet.

Methods of production of guns and ammunition have become much more sophisticated over the years. Companies such as Browning, Beretta and Remington produce production-line affordable guns of considerable quality.

A recent change has been the international adoption of one-ounce-load cartridges, though I feel that more must be done in the development of the cartridge particularly in relation to recoil and noise, to mention two of the issues. I suspect that the next 10 years will see some dramatic changes. Problems are there to be resolved, just as they were 100 years ago.

The other truly significant development of recent times has been the massive growth of interest in 'English' sporting, as it has become known. Up until 1980, trap shooting was the most popular form of clay pigeon shooting in the UK – now it represents just a fraction of shooters compared to those who shoot sporting clays.

Sporting with its variety, informality and challenge at all levels, has attracted a very broad cross-section of newcomers to the sport. It can be staged with no permanent fixtures. Layouts do not need to be installed so it is also inexpensive to put on. But it is the sheer variety and the shoot locations and imagination of organizers that have brought it to the fore. It offers competition for those who want to compete, it is fun for those who are looking for that and it has a similarity to live bird shooting that will appeal to the game shooter or hunter.

Sporting shooting has also been the basis for the boom in clay pigeon shooting as a vehicle for corporate entertainment. Targets can be presented as simple or as difficult as is needed for the standard of shooter involved.

There are now two sporting associations in the United States of America and a similar trend is emerging around the world. I am sure it will prove hugely popular.

2   My Shooting Career

I began shooting primarily because my grandfather was a gamekeeper. He was head keeper for Lord Weir on his grouse moor near Eaglesham in Scotland.

All four of my grandparents were true country people. My grandfather on my mother's side was a farmer whose land attracted a degree of notoriety on account of a very unexpected visitor. None other than Rudolph Hess made a parachute landing on to the farm following aircraft engine failure during the Second World War. He was subsequently captured and detained for the rest of his life. He landed on Castle Hill Farm, Eaglesham, owned by one John Young, whose name my father borrowed for the middle initial of my name – J. Y. Stewart was named after John Young.

So Eaglesham and the surrounding local comunity, whose livelihood was wholly based around farming, was very much part of my early upbringing. Although I spent only a small part of my life there, it is a very special place for me.

My grandfather on my father's side was one of those wonderfully elegant shots whose style could have been a study in how a gun should be addressed to the shoulder, how the arm should be held, and the swing be executed. A very elegant man, as so many gamekeepers can be. My grandfather therefore handed down this legacy to my father, who was a very keen shot all his life. Indeed his passion for shooting had obviously been fashioned by his upbringing in a gamekeeper's cottage, and in turn I too was brought up with guns being around my parents' home. We lived close to some excellent shooting. There was a grouse moor called Auchentorlie, which I am sure still boasts a stock of birds. In my father's day the moor was shot by a group of wealthy and successful businessmen headed by Mr Ronald Teacher of Teacher's whisky.

There was pheasant shooting on the banks of Loch Lomond on the estate owned by Sir Ivor Colquhoun who became a man legend for his many feats of strength and toughness. My father also enjoyed deer stalking high above bonny Loch Lomond. Indeed, most of the deer stalking by my father, my brother and later myself took place on a mountain called Ben Dhu whose base ran from Luss to Inverbeg.

The stalker was a wonderful man called Duncan McBeth who was the epitome of the Scottish deer stalker and perhaps more of a gentleman than any of the folk who he took to the hill to stalk the hinds and stags. He lived in a very modest picturesque cottage in Glen Luss. Duncan, like so many other people who were enormously important in the formative years of Jackie Stewart, was of country stock in the purest and best way.

My father kept his guns at home when in those days no safe or special compartments were required. He had a pair of Lancaster side-by-side shotguns which I well remember were easily identified by the brown damascus barrels. These were his guns for grouse and pheasant, and also the duck and geese that he shot in the same company as the grouse syndicate, again not far from Loch Lomond, near Gartocharn on ponds which in the winter provided sporting opportunities. For stalking, he owned a Mannlicher .275, which I still own today and it lives happily in Switzerland. It was by no means an expensive rifle, but ideal for the job.

Because grandfather Stewart lived in Lord Weir's keeper's cottage, called Netherhome, just outside Eaglesham, guns again were part of my early vision of Granny and Grandpa Stewart's wee wooden cottage. Their home was very comfortable with two bedrooms, a sitting-room (with a piano against one of the walls) and a kitchen which was used as the family room, with a big open stove that combined the role of cooker with being the house's only source of heat.

Outside were the kennels and the hen houses, but in the living-room was the gun case and this is where many of Lord Weir's guns were kept. There were Bosses, Holland & Hollands and a variety of others, all of course side-by-sides, some hammer-guns, most of them in pairs. It was a glass-fronted gun cabinet that might have been two and a half metres long; underneath were cleaning materials and various shooting paraphernalia. Cartridges were kept not in the house but in the outbuildings next to the kennels. It was a wonderfully primitive house where water had to be pumped up by hand and the lighting was by oil lamp. It had a telephone, however, as his lordship clearly needed to arrange shooting dates and other related matters with his head keeper. The phone was one of those wonderful pieces of apparatus that had an earpiece which you took off a hook and a little wheel you wound to connect with the operator; you then spoke into a separate mouthpiece which was attached to the wall. The whole thing was in heavy black Bakelite.

I have spent a lot of time at Eaglesham. I was born in 1939 when the war began and my mother's parents also came from Eaglesham, so I was sent away with my mother and my brother for a large part of the mid-to-late war years to avoid the bombing of the River Clyde. Our home was only five or six short miles from Clydebank, which at that time was one of the most important shipbuilding centres in Britain. The *Queen Mary*, *Queen Elizabeth*, the battleship HMS *Vanguard* and many other great ships sailed down the Clyde past our house on their way to greatness.

It was my father in fact who was to introduce me properly to shooting. He took me behind our house, which was called Rock View and was the place where I was born in the village of Dumbuck (now known as Milton), to Mr Bob

Crawford's farm. Here I was to get my first taste of pulling the trigger of a shotgun: he asked me to raise the gun to my shoulder and hold it in the correct firing position so that I could experience the bang and the recoil. I was only just a teenager, small and very slight of build – the recoil of the 32-inch-barrel 12-bore Lancaster was something that I wasn't quite ready for! We did not have a 20-bore or a ·410 in the house.

After recovering from that I was put to work on a turnip which my father let roll down a steep hill. While it bounced and rolled I was to attempt to shoot it. He had chosen the ideal spot which did not allow the spent shot to go anywhere other than into the bare bank. I practised this over and over again and it was clearly visible when you hit or missed the turnip. It was without doubt an excellent and highly innovative form of practice. A simple idea which taught me much.

Only after achieving a level of proficiency at this, was I allowed to have the privilege of shooting a clay pigeon from a hand trap, which I am sure he had borrowed from Grandfather Stewart. I was, at that time, 14 years of age. I recollect that I was able to shoot twice a week, but only under the supervision of my father or one of his friends who would work the trap, or take me to Eaglesham to shoot rabbits and pigeons which were classed as vermin, and they took careful note of my gun handling. Safety was stressed to me in such a way that, even as a youngster, I fully appreciated its importance.

I became more proficient as time went on and found a friend in Gordon Cameron who worked on Robert Crawford's farm. Gordon had already taken up clay pigeon shooting, together with his brother Hugh, and they told me all about it. The Cameron brothers lived in Dumbarton, a town that was famous for building the *Cutty Sark* in Denny's shipyard under the watchful eye of the Dumbarton Rock and for being the home of the famous

Ballantine whisky. Our family bungalow was one mile
away, adjacent to the garage which my father had built with
his own hands. This was the home in which, as I have said, I
was born, and where I lived until I was married at 23 years
of age.

It was Gordon Cameron therefore who took me to my
first ever clay pigeon shoot, held on New Year's Day and
run by the Gartocharn Gun Club, close by Loch Lomond.
Like so many gun clubs it had its good times and its bad.
Recently, I was very pleased to hear that the club has been
revived and is active once again. The participants on that
cold and wintry first day in January were mainly farmers
and keepers, rural folk with the odd exception such as one
very successful timber merchant called Tommy Anderson
who used an over-under. It was my first sight of such a gun.

The event was shot over trap (or down-the-line, as it is
now known). There were two traps and a pool trap, which
we shot in turn, and if you missed one target you were
eliminated. The main prize for the highest aggregate of the
day was a handsome solid silver trophy, which, lo and
behold, I won. I often look back and blame that day for the
enormous expense that the sport in later years was to be
responsible for in the Stewart economy!

Although I might not have wanted to recognize it at the
time, probably the only reason that I did win was because
the Scots are well known around the world for their manner of celebrating the arrival of the New Year. The shooting ground, therefore, was almost certainly filled with a
large majority of shooters whose finer reflexes were dulled
by the effects of festivities which had been in full flight
only hours earlier. Their judgement and accuracy may not
have been at their best. Nevertheless, I was the winner and
took home a variety of different awards and prizes, from
beer tankards to biscuit barrels and bottles of whisky.

Because the sport was so little known at that time I had
never seen a clay target being shot prior to my father introducing me to the experience. But I can well remember

being impressed by the spectacular effect of seeing them shatter in the air. If I were to think back, I related these incredible sights to the silver screen in the film *Annie Get Your Gun*.

The satisfaction of being able to do it myself and to see such evidence of the clay target being broken, even mildly or into dust, was to be an everlasting one. So, therefore, after the big success of the Gartocharn Gun Club competition, I was clearly going to be doing as many clay pigeon shoots as was humanly possible during 1956.

I had played soccer fairly successfully in the school team and had played for my county. School in general, however, had been a total disaster – I suffered from a learning disability which has now been identified as dyslexia. My schooldays had unquestionably been terribly unhappy with all the embarrassment and humiliation of incompetence in comparison to my peers. Shooting was therefore in a way a lifesaver for me. It gave me the opportunity to prove that I could do something as well as, if not better than, almost anyone else.

In those days to have a 14- or 15-year-old participating against grown men was rare, especially in Scotland. To have tasted some success was all the more rewarding – indeed it was like an infectious bug that I had been bitten with. I went to Taynuilt and Fasnaclough, to Stirling and to the Borders of Scotland, in other words I went anywhere I heard that a clay pigeon shoot was being held.

Gordon Cameron, and later on another keen shooter from Dumbarton called Andy Thompson, were my purveyors of travel. I was, of course, too young to drive a car or ride a motorcycle, but my father had a garage and therefore the odd gallon of petrol helped encourage them to go to shooting events.

I was to win a number of trophies in 1956 and I remember my Christmas card of that year being specially drawn by my family in an amateur but endearing fashion – I was depicted in a little caricature standing with my gun and surrounded by my prizes. Accompanying the drawing were the names of all the shoots that I had been to during the year.

The next step was to shoot for Scotland. This was a very big honour for me and to represent my country was something I had never previously dreamed of. The Scottish team was a 30-man squad, competing in an international match held annually and hosted in turn by each of the four 'home' nations – Scotland, England, Ireland and Wales. There never seemed to be a very defined procedure of selection in those days but the Scottish Clay Pigeon Association and its leading lights were clearly responsible for my call-up.

As I progressed, my father bought me a new gun: because of my size and weight and with the best intentions, he chose a light side-by-side. It was an Alex Martin ribless, a gun I still have. The recoil was vicious and if I grew up with fairly hefty shoulders it was probably because of my Martin ribless!

It was not until 1957 that I was to invest in an over-under, a Browning A1 bought from Brett Huthart at the cost of £119. It had a pistol-grip stock, which was supposedly of trap specification though I very much doubt that it actually was, for I was constantly having to build it up with Sellotape and bits and pieces of *Woman's Own* magazine to get the comb height to where I felt it was appropriate for my clay target shooting.

I had shot with some other guns in the meantime. One was a 30-inch Boss side-by-side belonging to my father, to which we had added a cross-milled raised rib (and as a consequence I am sure for the cost of £40 we totally destroyed Boss and Company's beautifully balanced gun!)

By 1957 I had left school, much to the relief of Dumbarton Academy and J. Stewart! I was 15 years of age and had little or no education to show for the pain and suffering. My father had financed my guns until then. As

I was working in the family business, money wasn't exactly plentiful. When I left school I was making £3 12s 6d a week, but was doubling that with tips from my job serving petrol and looking after the forecourt. So my shooting was being paid for by my earnings at the garage or, to be more precise, what was actually left after I gave my mother half of my wage packet. Needless to say it was a delicate financial balancing act and with the amount of shooting which I was beginning to do, plus the added cost of travel and accommodation, it was still necessary for my father to help me with my shooting.

In those days I was shooting Eley number 7 cartridges and with the amount of practice I was putting into it there were a few empty boxes lying about the house. In the days of my side-by-side shooting I stood in awe watching the skills of the great names of Scottish clay pigeon shooting at that time – Abe Bruce from the Borders, Tommy Bochie from the same part of the world, Bullseye McClelland, Bill Lowden, Tom Watson (who had a Rover car dealership in Kelso), Willie Manson from Argyllshire, Bob Love who seemed to be a gentleman shooter. Not forgetting Tom Simm, who like Bullseye and Bill, was a gamekeeper. To my dying day I will remember those people as being a major influence during the formative years of Jackie Stewart. I was driven to try to keep up with them and was enormously flattered if ever I beat them.

I was also seeing parts of Scotland that I had never heard of before, being driven along roads which wound their way through some of the most beautiful countryside in the world. I sat back taking it all in from the comfort of Gordon Cameron's Vauxhall Velox, a car which had more decorations and accessories on it than any Christmas tree in even the glitziest Fifth Avenue store. This was a car which was unmistakable. It had mascots on the hood, embellishers on the wheels, bug deflectors, exterior sun visors, and more wing mirrors and fog lamps than a Mexican taxi. Gordon shot an automatic Browning five-shot, as incidentally, did Bill Lowden, while Bullseye and Tom Simm shot conservative side-by-sides.

As my experience increased and time passed so I was introduced to speed. Andrew Thompson, another Dumbartonian who with his shooting pal Louie Barrett used to take me to shoots, had by this time purchased a Ford Zephyr. With its Raymond Mays conversion this was a car which would have frightened the most experienced racing driver with its fierce acceleration giving the effect of stripping all three of its gears, while laying down long strips of rubber on the road.

By then I had also been introduced to shooting in the south. I would travel down to Carlisle on the train, then go on with Brett Huthart, who at that time worked for Castrol selling lubrication bays and oil to garages around the north of England and south of Scotland. He was a keen shot who was a great aficionado of guns and for that matter the good life. A bachelor who lived with his parents in a small cottage south of Carlisle, Brett was to go on to become an Olympic shot for Great Britain and win many major events. He became very much a part of my life from the end of 1956.

He was to introduce me to a family who not only contributed a great deal to my shooting career but also proved a great influence in many other ways. Through Brett I met Glynne Jones, a wonderful man who was very successful in business – coming from a family of 13 he had created his own wealth from scratch. Glynne invented the Jones baler which at one time was the most sophisticated piece of agricultural baling equipment in the world. After a number of years of very successful production it was eventually bought out by New Holland. Glynne and his entire family were enthusiastic shots with considerable skill. He and his brother David both shot for Wales – they each had two sons, and all four also became excellent shots.

Glynne's sons, Noel and Allan, were in fact much later to become my partners in the Gleneagles Jackie Stewart

Shooting School. Those early days were really the formative years of Jackie Stewart: having come from the frustration and humiliation of my learning problems at school, I
was now getting a grasp on life and achieving some success.
I also met other people at this time who were to have a very
strong influence on my future. At that time I could foresee
only my shooting, along with my work in my father's
garage, but when Glynne Jones took me under his wing I
learned a great deal about life, the process of thinking, the
seriousness and the concentration associated with competition, and the dedication necessary to achieve success at all
levels of life.

I learned how to win and also how to lose. At one
moment you would be on top of the world shooting in a
totaly natural fashion, killing every clay target you shot at
almost by instinct, and winning events. However, the
moment that you started to believe you would always be
that good you got well and truly beaten and you also had to
take that with some dignity. When I look back, I sincerely
believe that my shooting days had a tremendous effect on
what was to happen later in my life with regard to my
motor racing career.

I remember driving everywhere in my brand new Austin
A30 – its registration number was ASN 500 and it was a
distinctive spruce green with Stewart tartan seat covers
and it had lots of chrome! It sat in the showroom of my
father's garage being wax polished time and again prior
to me even having a provisional licence to go out with
L-plates. One of the very big moments of my life was to
pass my driving test and secure my licence.

I began to travel the country from tip to toe. My driving
licence gave me a new freedom to travel on my own and go
to events that did not depend on Gordon or Hugh
Cameron, or Andy Thompson or Brett Huthart for that
matter. All of them played a tremendously important part
in enabling me to get into shooting at an earlier age than
most young people, while my father supported me with

invaluable financial help as well as moral encouragement.

One of my first big trips was to travel to the West of England Championships in 1956/7 at Blandford, where I won the doubles competition with 40 pairs straight. This was a score which stood for a very long time as a record in the United Kingdom. I think I finished third at the single-barrel championship at the same meeting.

I was then shooting reasonably well. It was just after that I began to shoot for Scotland, getting my first 100 straight, after of course having a 25-straight IMI patch which I sewed on my shooting jacket. I also got my 50-straight badge. And finally after what seemed to be endless waiting I got the famous 100-straight silver badge with pin that with great pride you put on to your shooting jacket along with the sew-on patch that came with the magic hundred. It was a blue badge with yellow writing. I still have it today.

Those were important landmarks in my life. I was to go on and win the Scottish Championship, the English, the Welsh and the British. I progressed from down-the-line to shooting ball trap (or continental, as it was then known) up on the mountain at Rhosesmor in North Wales, just a few hundred yards from where I would live when I stayed with the Jones family, who provided me with a base from which to travel for my competitive shooting. They were a fantastic family – Glynne and Hazel were two of the nicest people you could ever hope to meet, and Glynne was a great leader of men, who gave me encouragement whilst remaining my firmest critic.

Allan and I used to rush about the country in exotic motor cars. Being in the motor trade I used to pick up Jaguars from the factory and bring them to the Joneses' – if there was a good used car I would borrow it for the weekend to come down and stay while a shoot was going on. In the winter there was a shoot at North Wales every single month and of course in the summer many more competitions to go to. Noel Jones at that time was studying in the United States of America. Allan in his most glamorous years was driving a white 190SL Mercedes which was certainly one of the most appealing cars in North Wales.

We used to drive to Rhyl to meet at the cafés in the 190SL or an Austin-Healey or whatever happened to be available – and many a black mark was left on the road between Rhosesmor and the coastal resorts of North Wales. The same can be said for the road north from the Chester area back up to Dumbarton. I knew the road like

With my life-long friend and mentor,
Glynne Jones

the back of my hand, I knew every braking distance and every gear change, and in those days of course there were no speed limits on the roads, so while I was seriously becoming almost totally committed to shooting I was also learning a lot about driving.

It is often said that the reflexes which were evident in my shooting also had much to do with my skills at driving. I suppose that this is true, because if you shoot you have to be able to gauge speed accurately and read trajectories and angles clearly; you need excellent judgement and timing and you certainly depend on good hand–eye co-ordination, all of the things essential to a racing driver. You also have to learn to concentrate for long periods of time without making a mistake, Of course, when you make a mistake in a racing car it can be painful as well as expensive. But in a trap shooting competition when you make a mistake you can never buy back the loss of that target. From that point on your score can never be more than 99 out of 100, no matter how brilliantly you shoot. Another miss and you know that your total might never be good enough to win. This in itself was tremendous training, as I learned the need for self-discipline and sheer concentration in order to avoid mistakes. I also learned not to flake out under pressure.

The next step was Olympic trap, which in effect is to shooting what Formula One is to motor racing. It is the fastest, most difficult, most demanding and most competitive field.

Glynne Jones and his brother David installed Britain's first commercial Olympic trap layout at the North Wales Shooting School in Sealand, near Chester (though just in North Wales!). There is still a splendid photograph in the clubhouse at the ground taken at the time of that first competition on the new layout, which was also the first competition of that discipline in the UK. Some well-known faces of shooting are recorded there – Teddy Fear, Ted Saunders, Tommy Jones, Brett Huthart, Glynne and David Jones and a small and very young Jackie Stewart.

The first Olympic trap competition held in Britain was at the North Wales Shooting School in 1958 with 24 competitors and 12 staff. This photograph records the great men of British shooting who were present on that historic occasion: Standing: (*sixth from left*) Tommy Jones; (*eighth*) Teddy Fear; (*thirteenth*) Barney Mullen; (*sixteenth, in the white cap*) Allan Jones; (*eighth from right*) Ted Saunders; (*fourth*) Brett Huthart; (*third*) Harry Brunt; (*second*) David Jones; (*far right*) Clarrie Wilson;
Kneeling: (*fourth from left*) Freddie Nixon; (*seventh*) a very young Jackie Stewart; (*ninth, wearing sunglasses*) Glynne Jones

In the early days people were winning Olympic trap competitions with 85s and 87s out of 100. That crept up to 90 or a 92, later to be a 95 or a 97, but never 100 straight. Unquestionably, because Olympic trap was the most difficult, it was also the most satisfying. I think I rarely shot down-the-line (American trap) again. It now seemed so predictable – you could read all the angles and it simply wasn't challenging. I had shot from 16 yards at down-the-line, I had shot handicap by distance, and single-barrel and double rise and then gone on to continental and finally got to Olympic trench. I had no desire to go back down the ladder.

Allan and I then started to travel around Europe together shooting Olympic trap (or trench, as it was then known) competitions. My first trip abroad was to Paris to shoot in the European Championships in the Bois de Boulogne. One of the best French competitors of that time was Claude Foussier, who was a leading official with FITASC, the governing body of the sport at that time. He also shot for the French Olympic team. I was to become friends with Claude much later in life. He was a key figure in the Ricard drink company and brought Coca-Cola into France, and though he was already a very rich man, he went on to become even more successful in later years.

Allan Jones and I rented Vespas to get around Paris, which looking back was a very brave and somewhat foolish thing to do considering the risk involved in driving on the wrong side of the road and at the speed of the Paris traffic. We were staying near the Etoile and had to weave in and out of the densest traffic at the busiest times of the day to get to the Bois de Boulogne to do our shooting.

I had never shot abroad and the conditions were very hot. In fact I fainted at one point on the shooting ground, walking from number five to number one shooting position. Every time the gun went off my head exploded (not literally, but it very nearly felt that way). It was a terrible experience, but it was my first overseas championship and therefore a very memorable one.

We later went on to shoot abroad again in Geneva in 1958 in the European Championships where in fact I did quite well – not finishing close to the top ten but putting up a pretty good performance. In 1959 I believe the championship of Europe was shot at Monza, with the entire Italian team present, full of glamour and spirit. Liano Rossini, Franco Piatti, Gigi Rossi, Carlo Del Ventisette and Matarelli were amongst the shooters I remember instantly by name. We shot against the Russians, East Germans, Czechoslovaks and other teams from around the world. Maurice Tebat, from Lebanon, was very successful at that time.

When at Monza I had my first look at the famous autodrome. Carlo Delventesetti had a glamorous Alfa Romeo which we drove around the track. John Surtees was there while still a motorcycle racing champion riding for MV-Agusta. I remember him arriving in his sports coupé BMW – very smart, and very big-time.

In 1960 I went to the World Championships at Oslo driving a dark-blue 3·8-litre Jaguar with chrome wire wheels and beige upholstery, a magnificent car that was the family business's demonstrator. Goodness knows who I was promising to sell the car to on the ferry from New-castle to Oslo. Allan and I shot well in that event. I think I posted tenth best score in the World Championships that year and I was by then shooting to a high level at Olympic trap. We drove down from Oslo through Europe to Berne for the European event and I again placed well, returning to Britain to win several of the national championships that year.

I had already won the Coup des Nations in 1959 and again in 1960; I also won the British Grand Prix, along with the Welsh Grand Prix at North Wales and the Eng-lish at Bisley. I was as good at that time as I suppose I could have been and it was also the year of the Olympics.

The Olympic trials were run over a series of events through the winter months and on my twenty-first birth-day in June the final event was held at Beverley Gun Club in Yorkshire, the home of Joe Wheater. In those days Joe was a magnificent shot; fast and furious, he was an amazing man who seemed to fall out with most folk. Looking back, he might have been his own worst enemy because I think that Joe Wheater could have done a tremendous amount not only for himself but also for British shooting. He was such an artist with a gun.

He was leading the trials comfortably and I was in second place, also by a comfortable margin, and therefore looking to secure a place to go to Rome in the two-man Olympic team. Although I had been shooting for Great Britain and was proudly wearing the badge on my blazer, the Olympic rings were the biggest thing in my life to go for. In retrospect I am not at all sure I would have been good enough to have contended for a medal in the Olympics. But the honour of representing my country walking round that Olympic stadium for the opening and closing ceremonies was something that I had always dreamed of.

In 1959, aged 20, I won
the Coupe des Nations –
I am pictured here at the
North Wales Shooting
School with my friend
and rival in that
competition Mohedine
Natour of the Lebanon

On the very last trial on that twenty-first birthday I had one disastrous round where I missed eight targets out of 25. I completely lost my timing. I had no account for it but as a result I lost my place in the Olympic team by one target to Brett Huthart. It was the only real off-day I had had in 18 months. I had won almost everything that could be won in the UK and I represented the country well in overseas events but the selection method was perfectly clear. I simply fell apart at the wrong time.

I think that that was probably the biggest disappointment of my life as it was something which meant so much to me at a very young age. I was later to lose the Indianapolis 500 and I ran out of petrol on the last lap of the Belgian Grand Prix while leading. A variety of different motor racing disappointments came my way, including losing the World Championship in 1968. However, nothing I believe meant anything like as much to me as that precious day in Beverley when I threw away a chance to go to Rome. It was a tremendous lesson for me and I went on that year to win more events and I suppose from theat point of view it was satisfying that I was able to prove that I could come back and win. But nevertheless it didn't change the system of selection.

The following year we went to Spain to shoot in the European Championships in Barcelona. By this time I was getting on in years – 23 years of age, in fact! I had decided that this was the year when I would marry Helen, who is still my wife today (which I am told is pretty remarkable considering the kind of life that I live!).

We got married on 28 August 1962, and I think that I won the British Grand Prix that year and then decided to retire from competitive shooting. I could no longer afford both shooting and marriage, and therefore it was better to stop while I was still enjoying it. Looking back I feel that the decision was a very good one, probably as good a decision as I was to make later on in life when I retired as a Grand Prix driver, again before I had lost the love and flavour for that sport.

But economics also certainly played a large part in that decision of 1962. I did not give up game shooting but I reduced my activity in that also. I did, however, take up driving racing cars. From that moment on I pretty much dedicated my life to my motor sport and my family, and also I suppose to my work in the family garage. By the time I retired from shooting I had started to do a small amount

At the age of 23 I retired from competitive shooting while I still enjoyed the sport – this is a picture of me in 1962 having won the Welsh Grand Prix

of amateur club racing in the Borders of Scotland at Charterhall, not very far from where I had come to shoot clay pigeons, and close to where the great Jim Clark had his farm. From that point on I was unable to devote a great deal of time to any form of shooting. I still did a bit of salmon fishing, however: just as I had been brought up with a gun in my hand, I also had a great interest in fishing, particularly river fishing in the north of Scotland. Sometimes I was fortunate enough to go with my father to a stretch of the River Spey near Aberlour. This kept me close to the shooting fraternity and every now and again I would run into my old pals in one location or another.

I had been a mechanic in my father's garage preparing racing cars for a wealthy young enthusiast from Glasgow called Barry Filer. His family had not allowed him to race because of a family trust. He consequently had other people drive his cars that I prepared. Because of the time and commitment I gave to their meticulous preparation he rewarded me with the opportunity to drive one of his cars in a small event. I managed to do well and he asked me back to do more. From there it was one exciting offer after another, and shooting drifted away from me as I became totally submerged and intoxicated by a new love.

My motor racing developed very rapidly. I started to win pretty consistently at club level, and it then became necessary for me to travel south and do a tremendous amount of club racing. In 1963 I did 23 events, winning 14 of them. By 1964 I did 53 events, winning 23 in 26 different racing cars – quite a difficult thing to do. I was driving every kind of car of good quality that I could get my hands on. Small GT cars like Lotus Elans, Lotus Cortinas for touring-car events, Cooper Monacos, Tojeiro-Buicks, E-type Jaguars, even a 120 Jaguar in a historic race.

I then went on to Formula Three cars, Formula Two and even by the end of 1964 a Formula One car. It was my big year establishing myself in a new sport. My good fortune gave me four different offers to go into Formula One

Grand Prix racing for factory teams. The bug that had bitten me in my early shooting days when travelling all over Europe to shoot had caught me again because motor racing meant a different location and a different race track (and as time progressed, a different country) almost every weekend. The difference, however, was that instead of paying for my accommodation and buying my guns (although getting my cartridges for nothing) I was getting paid well for my racing.

World Championship Formula One racing started for me on New Year's Day in 1965 in East London, South Africa, for the South African Grand Prix. I was to meet up with many of the folk who had already become friends in my shooting days. By the time I reached the Italian Grand Prix at Monza I was being declared the new golden boy of racing. Half of the Italian shooting team turned up for the Grand Prix at Monza in the same royal park where I had come to shoot back in 1959. I remember well Carlo Del Ventisette and Gigi Rossi coming to several of my grands prix over the years. I was able to win the Italian Grand Prix that year, my first year in Grand Prix racing, 1965. I finished third in the World Championship, better than I had ever done behind the trigger of a gun!

By 1969 Monza was again to play an important part in my life for it was there in September that I clinched the World Championship for the first time. In 1970 Beretta presented me with a very beautiful pair of game guns which I still have today and almost always use for my game shooting. By then I had started to shoot again because of the many very kind invitations I had for pheasant shooting, grouse and partridge in Spain, Italy and Britain. So I was shooting in Scotland and England as well as Spain and Italy, where at that time there was very good pheasant and duck shooting.

I remember an incredible day's shooting in Manfredonia just north of Naples where I was the guest of the Manfredi family who owned the Baschieri & Pellegri cartridge company. We stayed in a unique shooting lodge which was built in a totally circular fashion with 12 guest suites all looking out on to a paradise for migrating duck travelling from northern Europe to Egypt. The interesting thing about that trip was that I arrived with a pair of Boss side-by-side round-action guns which I still own today. I was promptly told that I should shoot with the two-shot automatic Berettas that were being supplied to all the guests. The reason for this was that the hides that we were being taken out to by punt were concrete tubes sunk into the marshland (the bottoms of the hides had heated floors). It was de luxe shooting, but using an over-under or side-by-side you would almost inevitably have damaged the barrels of the guns as you broke them for reloading. So the automatic was chosen as the ideal weapon for the job. I have never been very fond of automatics, either the way they look or the sound they make. And in those days it simply wasn't socially acceptable. However, having said that, I found that I could shoot well with these guns. But there was definitely no temptation to use one afterwards – I have never used one since and have no intention of doing so.

Since my retirement from motor racing I have been fortunate to visit some of the finest shoots around the world. I find that I live to an incredibly busy schedule which involves much travelling, but in the autumn and winter months nothing gives me greater pleasure than to return to my native Scotland for either the grouse or pheasant.

The interesting thing about shooting is not only that it is a thrilling sport but also that it provides a wonderful safety valve. I think this is perhaps why it appeals to so many people from all walks of life. On a day's shooting in the middle of a Scottish moor or on the Sussex Downs it is almost impossible not to detach yourself completely from day-to-day pressures, whilst at the same time enjoy the relaxed company of others. There really is nothing quite like it.

3 The Gun

The first gun that I owned was given to me by my father and came from a prestigious Glasgow gunshop. It was called an Alex Martin ribless, and I have that gun to this day. It was felt that I should have a gun that I could easily carry and use, and of course the lighter it was the better proportioned it would appear in relation to my own somewhat diminutive physique. Moreover, on this particular model Alex Martin had had the brainwave of removing most of the rib, thus further reducing the weight.

The gun was definitely lighter than anything I had used before, but unfortunately this caused it to kick like a mule. I can recall many times coming home from clay pigeon shoots with my shoulder black and blue and, as a I progressed to events that were held over more than one day, I occasionally drew blood.

In those days there was not the same amount of information available to suggest what I might have done to

The first gun I owned was an Alex Martin ribless – light and manageable for the wee Stewart but with a kick like a mule!

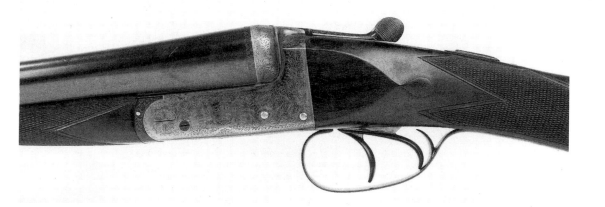

overcome the problem. This has obviously changed today and there are now many publications from all around the world that deal with the finer points of gunfit, technique, recoil, and so on.

I certainly didn't know about recoil pads back then. I used the same cartridges as other shooters did, and somehow took the battering as part of the privilege! The gun of course was very barrel light, so I used to get on to the targets very quickly and, because of my youthful exuberance, it seemed to work. This was one of my keys to success. The clay target would hardly rise from the clay pigeon trap by the time I would be shooting at it and in the large majority of cases blowing it to smithereens. In hindsight I suppose it must have looked as though I was showing off but it didn't occur to me at the time. This was the only way I knew how.

However, it was clear from what other people were telling me that the Alex Martin was not the ideal trap gun since it was definitely not designed for that purpose in the first place.

The next gun to arrive on the scene was a 30-inch barrelled Boss side-by-side. It was a lovely gun, beautifully balanced and with a fantastic single-trigger mechanism. It had tight chokes in both barrels and, because of what some of the successful trap shooters had been telling my father and me, we got Alex Martin's gunsmith to fit a very heavy file-cut raised rib to its 30-inch barrels. In fact, at a stroke we totally destroyed the above-mentioned wonderful balance, but it became for me a much more accurate clay target gun. I was to do well with it.

In the end, like all successful and consistent clay pigeon shooters, I had to go over to an over-under. This was bought with my father's help. As mentioned earlier it was arranged through a great friend of mine called Brett Huthart, a very knowledgeable and successful shooter, and a regular England and Britain team member.

The gun was a Browning A1 over-under trap gun which

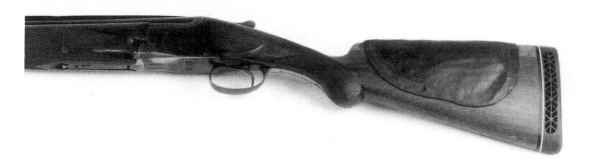

My faithful Browning A1 over-under trap gun, with its much-mutilated stock

in 1957 cost me £119. It had a semi-pistol grip and supposedly a trap stock. The barrels were 30 inches long with full and three-quarter choke, and a barrel selector on the safety-catch which was made for competition and therefore did not go 'safe' when the gun was opened. I also still have my Browning today with its much-mutilated stock. The look of the stock might be an embarrassment to some people, but not me. Goodness knows how many cartridges that old A1 has fired but it kept going and never really let me down – the most serious thing ever to go wrong with it being an ejector spring breaking perhaps only twice in its lifetime.

Brett assured me that this gun had a trap stock so I took his word for it, but, as I mentioned earlier, I then spent endless hours of building up the stock with reams of paper from my mother's *Woman's Own* magazines and using Sellotape to attach them to the varnished wood. I ended up with an incredibly high overview of the raised ventilated rib but for me it was to prove the perfect trap shooting configuration. The comb on the stock was much higher than anyone else could use, but I was to shoot American trap, or down-the-line (as it's known in Britain), ball trap and later Olympic trench with this gun. I bought a 'leg of mutton' gun case for it when I went to Barcelona to shoot in the European Championships in 1960. It was easier to carry even if it was not quite as protective a gun case.

My old Browning was eventually replaced by Beretta guns, which I used for both Olympic trap and game. But I have shot with a variety of different guns, especially for game shooting. From time to time I used my brother's Holland & Holland Royal, which was a single gun but a beautiful one.

In 1970, Ugo Gussalli Beretta gave me a beautiful pair of matching over-under game guns with magnificent wood and very mild engraving on the action. These are the guns that I still use today in preference to anything else, but now I am wise to the problems of its recoil and have pads and all the possible comforts fitted.

In 1970 I was presented with a pair of over-under game guns by Ugo Gussalli Beretta. These are the guns I use today in preference to anything else

One unusual characteristic of my guns dates back sadly to the time when I first took delivery of the Berettas when I went to shoot in Italy with Roberto Benelli in Tuscany. We shot for three days. High, sometimes unreachable pheasant shooting during the morning, followed by glorious long Italian lunches, and then on to shoot duck as the sun went down. The guns, however, had not been fitted for me, but were merely delivered to the Villa du Esté hotel in Cernobbio on Lake Como by Ugo Gussalli Beretta. This was for an official presentation photograph to be taken. I had won the World Championship for motor racing in 1969 and had known for many years the great Italian shooters who had shot for Beretta, like Liano Rossini, Franco Piatti, Carlo Del Ventisette, Gigi Rossi and another great Italian called Matarelli. A combination of the Italian love of fine guns and their appreciation of fast motor cars prompted Beretta to give this wonderful gift to the reigning motor racing World Champion.

When I went to shoot with Roberto Benelli, the Italians at that time used to shoot very harsh cartridges, even for game with about 1¼ ounces of load. The recoil with a gun that didn't fit me seriously damaged the blood vessels close to the surface of my chin bone, something that lives with me to this day. So therefore if anyone reading this book sees me shooting these days they will notice a recess has been cut out of the beautiful wood on the stock. The recess is filled with a sorbo insert that allows my cheek to sit tightly on the stock but not against the firm wooden stock itself. Sadly nowadays I cannot shoot without this kind of protection for after four or five shots my ruptured blood vessels enlarge to an extremely uncomfortable and unattractive lump – within 25 or 50 shots I will most likely break the skin and draw blood. The sorbo insert, however, works a treat.

I have, as a matter of interest, tried doctor after doctor to find a solution for this malady. I went to Muhammad Ali's doctor, Ferdie Pacheco, thinking that he might have a

special treatment for my chin but he told me that with a
surface injury such as this I should consult a plastic surgeon
or cosmetic specialist. So I visited a friend whom I shot
with at Lord Hambledon's estate in the Thames Valley
called Robin Baird. He was one of the leading specialists in
this field in the world having trained in the McIndoe Ward
at East Grinstead where the treatment of burns and scars
had been pioneered during the Second World War by Sir
Archibald McIndoe. However, at Robin's Harley Street
surgery, before I had completed my description of my
complaint, he interrupted me. 'My God!' he exclaimed.
'You don't have this problem as well, do you? I have had it
for years myself. It is incurable. I'm afraid you are just
going to have to live with it.'

So, if they couldn't change Stewart's face, they would
just have to change his guns. This I have done in a variety of
different ways but I have to say that Beretta have executed
this in a better fashion than anyone else. There was, however, a pair of very beautiful side-by-side round-action
single-trigger Boss guns which I bought from Glynne
Jones on which I never changed the stocks. I just put up
with the heavy bruising and the discomfort. Three years

Here you can see the sorbo insert
the gunsmiths at Beretta made for
my gun

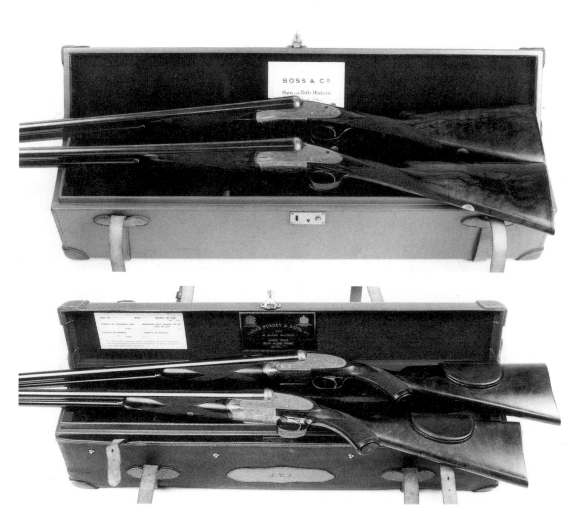

later I ordered and took delivery of a pair of Purdey 20-bore side-by-side guns. To overcome my chin problem Purdey attached a leather pad at the side of each stock to care for my tender face. It worked but didn't help the appearance of the guns which were, I believe, by far the most elegant I have ever owned.

I still have my pair of Boss round-actions and my 20-bore Purdeys. I fear I will never use them again but I know that they are both very good investments. And I have two sons who shoot, who I am sure will enjoy the privilege

Upper: On this pair of side-by-side round-action single-trigger Boss guns I never changed the stocks – I just put up with the bruising and discomfort
Lower: Purdey attached pads to my Purdey 20-bore side-by-sides – it helped my face but it didn't do anything for the appearance of these beautiful guns

In 1989 Beretta gave me a very special gift: a new model called the ASE 90 with beautiful engravings of the three Formula One racing cars with which I won the World Championships

of using these elegant, artistically engineered guns, beautiful examples of craftsmanship which is seriously in danger of becoming a lost art.

I also have a Beretta trap gun. But in 1989 Beretta again gave me a very special gift. It was a new model called the ASE 90. In addition to being beautifully built, the gun was worked on by one of their most outstanding engravers who depicted the three different cars with which I won the World Championships. Using photographs as his source he brilliantly etched the cars with me driving them, one on each side of the action and the other underneath. I call it my Grand Prix gun.

I have owned a Merkel over-under for which I perhaps erroneously swapped the 30-inch side-by-side Boss that my father had given me all those years ago. The East German-made Merkel, although a good gun, could never have been called elegant or beautiful with its deep bold engraving on the action. Also, because so many people in Europe and Eastern Europe still carry shotguns with a strap over their shoulder, the gun had sling swivels. I promptly removed these in the interests of elegance! It was not a gun that I ever really felt comfortable with and in fact I sold it through the Jones family at the North Wales Shooting School.

Helen, my wife, owns a Beretta 20-bore over-under and like a great many women when she makes up her mind about shooting within a very short time she can be extremely accurate at clay pigeons over the sporting layouts that we have at Gleneagles.

I have never, however, been a great collector of guns. Like so many things in life, with twenty-twenty hindsight I can see my mistakes and that I should have collected more as an investment. Without really looking for them there have been many opportunities that have come my way during my travels, much in the same way as I would have been a much richer man had I collected any of the wonderful racing cars of my motor racing career.

Today I shoot with a great variety of people. The traditional game shot, the establishment figure, will most likely have a gun which has been handed down from generation to generation. These are always side-by-side English guns with clean 'straight' sporting stocks. Never pistol grip or semi-pistol grip, but with actions that are as smooth as silk, self-opening and well-used, they are usually 12-bore gauge, though sometimes 16-bore. A user of such a piece (if I recall correctly) is the Duchess of Devonshire. Many 20-bore shotguns are now used by men as well as women, mostly on a side-by-side configuration, although some today have over-unders.

I have also had the thrill of shooting with the best of my generation. One of England's greatest game shots was the late Sir Joseph Nickerson, whom I saw shooting beautifully with over-under 28-bores. In addition to creating a hugely successful business empire, Sir Joseph spent much of his adult life shooting. His knowledge of guns, game and conservation was exceptional. It may seem contradictory to some that he was a keen environmentalist and conservationist while still a keen shooter, but his book *A Shooting Man's Creed* underlines the compatibility of the two roles with wonderful clarity.

One of the finest exhibitions of shooting I have ever seen, however, was conducted by a man called Claude Foussier. As mentioned earlier, I had shot with Claude in the 1950s at the European Championships when he was an important member of the French team and was to become president of FITASC, at that time the world governing body of shooting. But I will never forget when I shot with him and the sight of Claude bringing down some of the higher pheasants I have seen killed at the Duke of Buccleuch's Langholm estate. I had not paid any attention to the guns Claude was using. It was only after I positioned myself next to him in the line following the draw for stands and when the shooting began that I realized that he was not using 12-bore cartridges. The difference in the sound of the detonation should have been the giveaway. I am sure that any shooter would have shared my feelings of tremendous surprise, and perhaps some shock, when I found out that he was using a pair of ·410 over-unders.

I had always thought that Claude was a fine shot but following that exhibition I likened him to a salmon fisherman

walking across the surface of a river to catch his fish. I have
told colleagues about this incident from time to time and I
am invariably accused of gross exaggeration, if not telling
downright lies. His shooting was all the more remarkable
as Claude also has a considerable disadvantage in that he
lost an eye in a shooting accident. Luckily for him it was
not his master eye, and it clearly does not drastically affect
his shooting.

In any shooting book or at any bar you will hear great
tales of the marksmanship, styles and ability of the greatest
game shots that the world has known. To this day there are
many who will speak reverently of the skills of Lord Derby,
Lord Ripon, some of the great Spaniards who have created
records in Spain, Europe and Britain. In modern times
names such as Sir Joseph Nickerson, the Duke of Roxburghe, Hugh Van Cutsem, Lord Stafford, one or two of
the Hambros and I am sure many others. My views on all of
those great shots is that, as in any activity, it is impossible
to be consistently perfect. There are many very good shots
who on their day are truly extraordinary.

So what types of gun do these wonderful shots use? Of
the above, very few would use anything other than side-by-
sides. In many circles it is still considered infra dig to come
to a shoot with anything other than an English gun of that
configuration. It is, of course, becoming less true today and
it is always amusing for me, who truly believes the over-
under to be the most suitable gun available, to see a game
shot changing over to an over-under to shoot clay targets.
Their easy answer is to say that normally they can shoot clay
pigeons more accurately with the over-under. However,
this is always difficult for them to justify: if they prefer an
over-under with a clay target, why is it then not more accurate with a game bird? Indeed, there hasn't been a serious
clay pigeon competition won in the last 30 years by someone using a side-by-side gun. In clay pigeon shooting
accuracy and consistency are a formula that is absolutely
paramount in the mind of the competitor. He chooses his

gun and his ammunition very carefully to attain the maximum benefit to achieve the near-perfect scores that are now essential for a regular front runner. The over-under has filled this role better than any other gun, although the semi-automatic and the pump-gun, particularly in the USA, have also been major players. The single plane of vision of the over-under or the single barrel seems to be the common denominator.

But it will, I think, take a good many years to remove the social-acceptance factor that represents such a significant part of field sports, manifested in people's dress, manners and time-honoured traditions. The side-by-side, particularly to the English, has always been seen as the most appropriate gun to arrive with at a shoot for a guest making his first visit. I have to admit that this was the only reason for me purchasing my own side-by-side Boss and Purdey guns. I had, of course, shot game as a young man prior to ever becoming a racing driver, but the number of invitations I received multiplied considerably as my motor racing career became successful. There were many shoots I went to where I am sure that the large majority of people expected me to arrive dressed in my racing overalls shooting with some illegal weapon with manners and etiquette that might have threatened their pleasant day out. I hope that I disappointed them. Grandfather and Father Stewart had drilled into wee Jackie how to behave, how to hold his guns, not to shoot other people's birds and to present himself in a manner that wouldn't embarrass either of them, even in their graves.

I have never been a keen wildfowler however. I suppose it must mean that I am a little soft, but then in my racing driving career I didn't much like driving long-distance races such as Le Mans and Sebring, which required sessions in the dark. Perhaps my eyes don't have the necessary depth of perception in failing light and are not suited to the challenge of flighting duck or geese, either early in the morning or in the evening. As a young man I used to go wildfowling on the Solway Firth with Glynne and Allan Jones. Having been brought up in Scotland, I was used to the damp and cold, but it gave me no pleasure and I think that after about two or three trips I found something else to do at the appropriate time.

I remember once seeing a most unusual gun in the hands of a very talented shooter called Lord Cawdor. It was a 10-bore and he used it for the purpose of wildfowling to bring down some high geese or duck. I daresay the biggest problem he had was finding ammunition for it. This great 10-bore was certainly substantial to look at, and heavy to hold. I never actually saw him shoot it.

Choosing Your Gun

Mass-production over-unders such as the Beretta 686 and Browning B325 are excellent guns for the money, and it is this type of gun which I would recommend without reservation to any newcomer to the sport. They are well-made guns which often appreciate in value over the years and will give the owner a lifetime's use. A gun of this sort will not wear out. We use the Beretta 686 and 687 at Gleneagles to fire an enormous amount of cartridges and they are in constant use. This would not be possible even with one of the very best London guns!

An over-under by one of the better-known makers will also handle extremely well, having been carefully designed to feel comfortable in your hands. They have more weight than the side-by-side and absorb recoil easily, but are well balanced so that the extra weight isn't at all noticeable. Moreover, the added weight is invaluable in keeping the muzzle steady for the second-barrel shot. Also the single sighting plane is without question a further advantage.

The side-by-side's lightness is only a benefit if you are likely to be carrying the gun all day. Users will tell you that

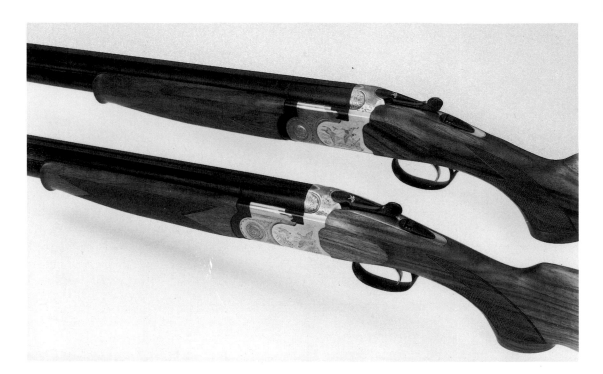

A pair of Beretta 687s – the gun we favour for our pupils at Gleneagles for its all-round versatility and durability

it is easier to load, but any advantage in this area is a trade-off to other disadvantages when actually firing the gun. I will not argue, however, that the side-by-side is not an excellent gun for pure driven shooting. But it is no better than the over-under which can perform better in other areas on different targets.

The Sporting Shotgun

I believe that it is vital for anyone involved in a sport to know about his equipment. With a basic understanding of a car engine it is possible to get more out of it, to play a decent game of golf you need to know when to use a 7-iron and when to choose a wood, and to shoot well you will find that by understanding gunfit you will improve your performance.

It is appropriate first to discuss the basic differences between the various bore sizes.

The ·410, the best-known among the small-bore shotguns available today, is the only gun which owes its name to the measurements of the diameter of its bores; that is, four-tenths of an inch. The names of other guns were arrived at in a somewhat different manner.

The original gunmakers were not in fact engineers, but medieval armourers. They measured the bore by the number of spherical balls of pure lead, each exactly fitting the interior diameter of the barrel, required to make up a total of one pound in weight. For example, a 20-bore requires 20 such lead balls, whilst a 12-bore requires only 12. Therefore the 20-bore has a smaller barrel than the 12. By and large, the big-bore shotguns that have found favour with wildfowlers are the 4-bore, 8-bore and 10-bore.

So what about the actual size of the barrel's internal measurement? The diameter is normally taken at around nine inches from the breech. Legally, every gun must meet the rules of proof in the country in which it is to be used. These rules are universal, if a little vague! On being passed fit for use by a Proof House, the barrels of a 12-bore, for example, are stamped with the figures ·719, ·729 or ·740.

So, you know exactly the internal diameter of the bore. There is, however, no specified minimum or maximum bore wall thickness. This is not a problem with any new gun, but an old gun may have barrel walls that have worn too thin. Gunshops will check the thickness with a gauge, but if you are buying an old English gun privately, this is something you must watch out for.

By far the most popular gauge is the 12-bore, its size being near perfect for all-round use and suitable for the vast majority of shooters. However, some game shooters looking for something lighter have in the past thought in terms of the 16-bore. Nowadays this gauge is becoming increasingly obscure, and the 20-bore has become much more popular. 'Sixteen' aficionados will claim that this gun is the ideal size, but its critics respond that it falls between two stools – it still being too big to be genuinely unrestrictive. Consequently, with fewer users, 16-bore cartridges are now harder to get hold of and very expensive. Twenty-bores, however, have really come into their own. Once the preserve of young boys and lady shooters, they are now a serious option for the discerning game shot. With modern cartridges, the 20-bore can hold its own under most game shooting situations.

My own particular preference, and still the popular choice, is the 12-bore over-under, which, if built by a good maker and of the dimensions to fit its owner, is without doubt the most versatile and effective shotgun on the market today.

THE PARTS OF THE GUN

When most of us go into any new sport we learn the hard way. We make basic errors along the learning path and we pick up habits which return to haunt us later in our careers. This is the reason why I feel that it is crucial to get a grasp of the sport under the watchful eye of an experienced coach. The good instructor will make sure that your gun fits you. It is impossible to shoot consistently well with an ill-fitting gun, so let's look at the fundamental points to remember.

The design of a shotgun is such that if it is properly fitted and held by the shooter correctly every time, with no conscious effort, then it will always give the same perfect view of the target when he is looking down the barrel. The shooter will ideally see just a little of the top rib, but when actually shooting all he will consider is the target. He will not be aiming the gun, as with a rifle, but pointing it as if he were pointing a finger at an object. The gun is, if you like, a surrogate finger.

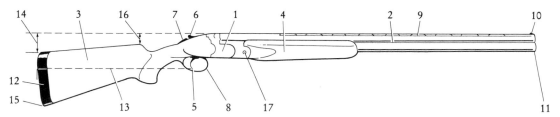

1 Action 2 Barrel 3 Stock 4 Fore-end 5 Trigger 6 Top lever 7 Safety 8 Trigger guard 9 Ventilated rib 10 Front sight 11 Muzzle 12 Butt plate (or recoil pad) 13 Stock length 14 Drop at heel 15 Toe 16 Comb height 17 Hinge pin

There are three principal areas of fit which are very important: the length of the stock (number 13, see diagram above), the comb height (16) and the cast (see below). All three combine together to assist the perfect gun mount. If the stock is of the right length, your cheek will rest on the gun approximately 1½ to 2 inches from the front of the comb. The comb height will be around the same measurement.

The cast will be decided by what we call the 'thickness' of the face. The stock can adjusted away slightly from the line of the barrels, thus allowing the master eye to look immediately down the rib for the left- and right-hander. There are some shooters who have a master eye problem; for instance, a right-hander with a left master eye. The solution to this, in my opinion, rather than having a cross-over stock (which is hugely contorted in order to present the rib to the 'other' eye), is to learn to shoot off the opposite shoulder.

A more common problem is that some people find it awkward shooting with both eyes open, which is without

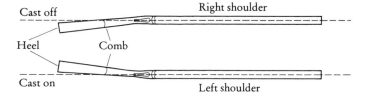

The cast can be tailored to suit an individual shooter's style of aiming

doubt the best method. If, for instance, a right-hander's right eye is not a total master, then it may be advisable for him to shoot with one eye closed. The best way of doing this is to keep both eyes open until the moment before pulling the trigger – this gives the overall perspective, but at the last minute brings the finer point into focus. Strangely, this is a problem experienced by many women.

Where possible, however, I would always recommend that both eyes be kept open throughout. As mentioned earlier you should be looking at the target, not aiming at it.

One other important tip is that when trying out a gun or having a gun fitted you should wear the same amount of clothing that you expect to be wearing for most of your shooting. Also remember always to mount the gun in the same spot in your shoulder as if you were actually shooting.

BARREL LENGTH AND WEIGHT

The ideal all-round barrel length is 27½ or 28 inches. This will be ideal for most sporting clays, skeet and game shooting. For the trap disciplines, however, I always shoot with a 30-inch barrel, which gives a little more 'pointability' on those long retreating targets, and tends also to have a stabilizing effect. The shorter barrel can be a little too lively for this kind of target. Many of the top sporting shooters now use 30-inch barrels – as the targets are thrown at greater ranges then the longer barrel really comes into its own. Some even use 32-inch barrels, which may be good in the right hands, but in my opinion are a handicap to the average shooter.

The weight will vary enormously depending upon the type of gun chosen. A side-by-side will be less than 7 pounds, but I would recommend an over-under of 7½ to 8 pounds. It is best to shoot with as heavy a gun as you can comfortably handle. As stressed earlier, a gun needs to be of sufficient weight to absorb recoil which both spares the shooter and gives you a smooth, steady swing.

Most shotguns balance on the hinge pin, though some of the modern multi-choke 30-inch guns tend to be a little muzzle heavy. There is conflicting opinion about this: some say that the heavy barrels spoil the balance of a gun, while others claim that a little extra weight at the muzzle keeps the gun on a steady line. My own preference is for a gun which is in fact perfectly balanced on the hinge pin.

Some game shooters will be seen to be using 25-inch barrels on side-by-sides. This barrel length was pioneered by Robert Churchill, a brilliant shot who did his gun-making business no harm whatsoever by advocating a style of shooting based upon his Churchill 25-inch gun. Some shoot very well with these guns. Others are inconsistent, and it's not hard to see why – with a short barrel the swing tends to be very quick, which is fine for fast-reflex shooting such as partridges and grouse, but not much of a help with high curling pheasants. And definitely not a gun for clay shooting.

OTHER POINTS TO REMEMBER

Triggers on modern guns tend to be of good quality and will be set up for pulls of around 3½ pounds on the first barrel, and 4½ on the second. If you have any doubts you should get them checked – cheaper guns can be notoriously bad with very heavy pulls that make it impossible for a shooter to translate his co-ordination into good shooting. Conversely, lightly set trigger pulls can be very dangerous.

I would always recommend that anyone taking up the sport should buy the best gun that they can afford. I don't mean that they should splash out on a Purdey, but look in the direction of a Beretta, Browning, Perazzi or any of the other well-known makes. These guns tend to be better made, more reliable and better suited to the specified discipline. And even a bottom-of-the-range model will hold its own in terms of price. If properly looked after, most guns will last a lifetime, and after five years' use they are often worth as much as was paid for them.

You will see, incidentally, that most makes produce over-unders in 'Game' (or 'Field') specification. I would recommend, however, that if you are buying a gun as an all-rounder you invest in a 'Sporting' model, that is one that has been designed specifically for sporting clays. The 'Field' guns are too light for truly effective clay shooting.

The shape of the fore-end will be a matter of personal preference. I always think that it is nice to have a gun that looks attractive, has well-figured wood and good engraving. You are much more likely to respect it and take care of it. It will become a part of you and this is very important if you have aspirations of shooting well.

Finally, multi-chokes (dealt with in more detail on pages 81–2) are nowadays available on most guns. This again is a matter of personal preference. There is no doubt that it is possible to shoot most clay targets and game with the standard fixed chokings of $\frac{1}{4}/\frac{1}{2}$, but the multi-choke gives you useful options. Moreover, as they are now well concealed within the muzzles of the barrel, they do not detract from the look of the gun. A multi-choke gun will afford you the option of shooting with open chokes for skeet and tightening them for trap. If you find that you like trap shooting, however, you will definitely need to invest in a specialist trap gun – more about that later.

SIDE-BY-SIDE

The side-by-side is probably the gun which springs to most people's minds (certainly non-shooters) if you mention the words 12-bore. This is because for many years the side-by-side was the only double-barrel shotgun and, despite the introduction of the over-under 70 years ago, there are still many who regard it as a 'new fangled thing'.

Certainly all of the crucial development of the shotgun was carried out on the side-by-side, the big breakthrough

coming in the 1850s with the breech loader. This set the
scene for a thousand patents and refinements, with the
sporting shotgun quickly evolving into a form to which
there have been few changes made in nearly 100 years.
Recent improvements have largely been restricted to ejector and locking mechanisms. It is in every sense a classic
design.

OVER-UNDER

The major breakthrough for over-unders came in 1926
when an extraordinary man called John Moses Browning
introduced the B25, a superb piece of engineering and a
model which is still on sale today virtually unchanged from
his original design.

The other classic design came in 1932 when Beretta
launched their SO, a sidelock-mechanism over-under
which again has had various small refinements but is largely
the same gun as when first introduced more than 60 years
ago.

The fifties saw the development of the over-under as a
competition gun. By the sixties and seventies the principal
makers in Italy and Japan had invested in sophisticated
machinery for the mass-production of these guns – they
were consequently able to produce high-quality guns at
affordable prices. English gunmakers, for so long the
world leaders in side-by-side manufacture, never really
recovered from the war. A decline set in which the industry
was unable to halt – Spanish guns were soon finding their
way on to the world markets. They copied the English
styles, and the best Spanish guns, such as the AYA, offered
very good value.

In the USA it is pleasing to note that Remington are still
in production and are highly successful, and that Ruger are
also doing very well. It is no longer possible, however, to
buy a new Winchester double-barrel shotgun. The manufacture of this classic was undertaken in Japan, but the

factory was sold and I am told that it is now the site of a golf course and car park!

Today relatively few guns are made in England. Purdey and Holland & Holland still manufacture very high-quality side-by-side sidelocks, and their guns are the most sought after in the world today. Hollands, who are now owned by French perfumers Chanel, are also in the process of introducing two new over-unders – a sidelock and a sporting clays gun. Hollands also own the W. & C. Scott factory in Birmingham where boxlocks are produced. William Powell of Birmingham still make a few very nice guns, but other than these there are just a few small specialist makers producing quality sidelocks for clients, such as Boss, Symes & Wright, Peter Nelson and William Evans.

BOXLOCK AND SIDELOCK

The essential difference between a boxlock and a sidelock is that the former has its locking mechanism housed within a box-shaped compartment in the end of the stock where the wood meets the metal, while the latter's working parts are built on to the inside of the lockplates on the side of the action. In general, the boxlock is one-tenth of the price of the sidelock. This is simply because the boxlock can be easily mass-produced, but the sidelock can only be made by hand.

The complex sidelock mechanism can only be made by hand

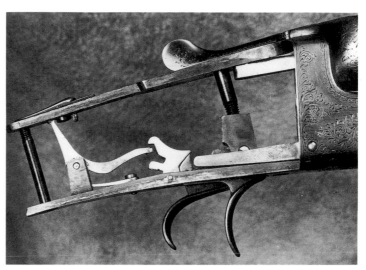

The boxlock of the Churchill, seen here with the stock removed, is a relatively simple mechanism and so can be mass produced

In practical terms, while there is no doubting that the sidelock is the more desirable and much more aesthetically pleasing of the two designs, a good-quality boxlock will do the job every bit as well, be the gun a side-by-side or over-under.

CLEANING YOUR GUN

An important discipline worth learning from the outset is always cleaning a gun after use. It's a simple job that doesn't take five minutes – in return you will have a gun that will most likely never let you down. Also, of course, make sure that you have somewhere safe and secure where it can be stored. This is a responsibility which should never be taken for granted.

There can be few tasks simpler than cleaning a shotgun. A cleaning rod, a spot of oil and a piece of cloth are all that is needed, plus a couple of minutes of your time. The rewards are considerable.

I go to a great many shoots where I am given someone to accompany me during the day to look after my guns and cartridges, and quite often at the end of the shooting they take my gun away and clean it for me. Of course, this is a very nice gesture and it enables me to immediately join my host for afternoon tea or refreshment. However, where possible I prefer to clean my own gun. It was something that I was brought up to do. My father quite rightly insisted that this was my responsibility, and with good reason. By doing it myself I am able to see if there is something which has altered from the last time I used it. By not only cleaning the stock and lubricating the various parts, but also removing the fore-end and looking at the gun closely, I will see any hint of a fault that may be developing. If there is anything different, a mark, a split in the wood or a separation of the rib from the barrels, I will notice it. Any hint of corrosion will be detected.

Nowadays we have aerosol cans of cleaning oil, but when I started shooting my father taught me to take a pigeon's feather, dip its tip in oil and run it on each side of the rib of the gun to make sure that there was oil right down into the finest point of the rib. This would stop any moisture or water seeping into unwanted places. I'm afraid that even the nicest of people wouldn't pay that kind of attention to someone else's gun. No guns are cheap, for they are built to last, and I am a great believer in cleaning my own gun after every occasion on which I have used it.

Also, of course, close care and attention will prevent accidents. Guns that are not properly looked after, with faults that have not been detected or with a build-up of dirt and corrosion, can be lethal.

SECURITY

I would always recommend that all gun owners invest in a security cabinet. We all have an obligation to prevent guns from falling into the wrong hands – and precautions such as cabinets provide 99 per cent of that prevention.

Additionally, it is better to keep guns in a cabinet where they can breathe than anywhere else.

Never leave a gun in a slip overnight, certainly if for

A gun security cabinet is essential

Upper: A Purdey sidelock, with its locking mechanism built on to the plate above the trigger
Lower: A Churchill boxlock has a compartment in the stock in which the boxlock mechanism is housed

some reason it hasn't been cleaned. If the barrels have been exposed to the wet (or even extreme cold) blacking on the barrels can become spotted with brown corrosion in a matter of hours. If left in a gunslip condensation can prove a real enemy.

So always, on returning home, take a couple of minutes to clean the gun and put it away in the cupboard.

Cartridges

Cartridges are to some people more important than guns. There are those who will only use one brand, one type, one load – as if their favourite brand is a lucky charm or a sort of comfort blanket. This can help confidence, but it's fairly true to say that today there are very few poor cartridges sold on the market. I dare say that many people would like to think that some, however, are better than others.

We in Britain tend to think that the continentals still like to shoot with heavier cartridges than ourselves. Snobbery leads people to think that it's unsporting, noisy and rather heavy on the shoulder. Matters of sportsmanship should not come into the argument, but the other elements surely do. In some cases the more traditional English guns would be unable to handle consistently the heavy-duty cartridges that are still available on the market. And it has now been proved that, unless the quarry is goose, there is no need for especially powerful ammunition – far better to have a lighter load of good quality.

I also feel that using the same load, and therefore the same speed of cartridge, allows you to get used to the kind of killing power that one can expect. Seldom is it the cartridge that is to blame, and almost never is it the gun, but sometimes the change of brand can rebuild a little confidence.

I myself now firmly believe in comfort. Maybe I am

getting too old, but I don't want to abuse myself any more with getting whacked on the shoulder each time I squeeze the trigger. With the wrong choice of cartridge it can be like being kicked by a mule. For example, at the Jackie Stewart Shooting School at Gleneagles we use a very light load of ⅞ ounce. This is the sweetest, softest cartridge that we can find. Our decision to opt for this load has been made because 60 per cent of our customers are first-generation shooters, and 40 per cent are women whose greatest fear is the recoil. Our cartridges are especially made for us and without question they help a great deal. The ammunition is still clearly good enough to break targets from our highest towers and our furthest disciplines, while supplying a softer sound and a more comfortable response to the pull of the trigger.

When I started my game shooting I always shot with Eley Grand Prix which was 1¹/₁₆ ounce. No. 6 shot was the chosen size, and No. 5 for duck. For clay pigeons I used 1⅛ ounce with 7 shot. When I moved on to shooting continental ball trap and Olympic trench I had to get used to shooting 1¼-ounce cartridges with 7½ shot. The most popular and successful cartridge amongst the big-time shooters was the Legia Star from Belgium or the MB from Italy. The Legia was certainly the smoother of the two. The MB had a sharper, faster recoil that used to give me second thoughts about pulling the trigger unless it was absolutely essential, particularly at the end of a long shooting day.

Eley then brought out a competitor to these loads in the early sixties, the Olympic trap with a 1¼-ounce load of nickel-plated shot. This cartridge at the beginning of its career also shocked the system pretty heavily, but in later years it became a very successful cartridge.

More recently the regulations have twice been changed: first the load was reduced from 1¼ to 1⅛ ounces, and now today in all the disciplines you are not allowed to shoot more than a 1-ounce load. Although it was initially thought that this would make a considerable difference to results, this has not been the case. The competition 1-ounce load has been developed considerably and the only shortcoming is that there are fewer pellets in the shot to reach out and hit those Olympic trench targets. Interestingly, the high level of competitiveness and professionalism in the sport has led to today's scores being just as high as those from the days of the heavier, noisier and more uncomfortable cartridges.

On the subject of recoil, I am a strong believer in eliminating as much of it as possible. I am no macho man. Why create a possible discomfort when you can eliminate it? It serves no useful purpose, in fact it can be of considerable detriment to performance and recoil can negatively affect the inexperienced shooter's chance of hiting a target with the second barrel. If the gun is not being held properly and the shooter's face is not correctly placed on the stock, an excess of recoil will make it almost certain that a novice will not recover the correct grip and have all of those important elements in place for the second barrel.

Modern materials have, however, considerably reduced recoil. When I started to shoot the only feasible way of achieving this was to attach a rubber pad which slipped over the stock. No one particularly wanted to shorten the expensive woodwork to attach an ugly rubber recoil reducer and it interfered with the gun comfortably coming to the shoulder of the shooter, causing the pad to catch on the clothing and make good gun mounting very difficult. Also a rubber recoil slip over the end of the stock is clearly going to change the dimensions of the stock for the shooter, potentially causing many more difficulties. Too long a stock can be just as much trouble in terms of both discomfort and inaccuracy as one that's too short.

If a shooter, man or woman, is properly introduced to the sport, with the correct amount of time and coaching, recoil should not be a problem in relation to discomfort. For the correct and most comfortable grip I always tell new shooters, if they are right-handed, to push their left hand

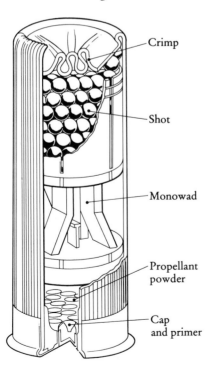

A modern cartridge

Crimp

Shot

Monowad

Propellant powder

Cap and primer

with fingers outstretched across their chest to the beginning of their right shoulder. Here you find what I call the 'sweet spot', which feels almost like a pocket that your fingers will be able to snuggle into. On the outside of the shoulder you can feel the bone is cushioned with little flesh. Likewise if you put the same set of fingers closer to the neck you run into your collar-bone, which again is relatively exposed with little padding to cover it. However, between the end of the collar-bone and the beginning of the shoulder bone there is a comfortable area where the stock of a gun can be placed which will allow no immediate contact with a heavily boned area. By raising the elbow of your right arm roughly to the height of your shoulder as if you are going to pull the trigger of an imaginary gun, you will find that the 'sweet spot' does in fact open out to give you even more room for the imaginary gun stock.

Having identified this area the shooter should then lift the gun to the shoulder and repeatedly place it in what he or she has identified as the comfort area. If the gun is always placed in this comfortable position, most people should be able to shoot 50 or 75 cartridges in a day, even as a beginner, without feeling shoulder pain.

At the Jackie Stewart Shooting School we help gentlemen of slight build and ladies in two ways. We can go to the 20-bore, which offers less recoil and is a much lighter gun or we can present a shooter with a heavier 12-bore gun which will absorb far more of the recoil. For a lady of not generous proportions, however, we would only suggest the 20-bore to start with, mainly because it is easier to lift to the shoulder and so particularly desirable during early shooting lessons as the instructor may ask the lady to hold the gun up at her shoulder for a little extra time to correct hand or head placements. Once that basic instruction has been carried out we would often change over to the 12-bore which on some occasions can be more comfortable to shoot, as long as light-load cartridges are used.

For some reason the cartridge business over the last 10 or 15 years has not spent much money on research and development in shotgun ammunition. We are therefore still using the same cartridges and the same theories about the materials and building of those cartridges which have now been around for a very long time. I would not suggest that there has not been any improvement but the acceleration level of technology has not been anywhere near as high as that in many other sports-related industries. This applies to the recoil, noise and the range of cartridges. I myself feel that a considerable amount could be gained if the gun and ammunition producers of the world pooled their resources and became determined to make some progress in these fields.

THE PATTERN

While I wouldn't wish to delve too deeply into the complexities of cartridge design and manufacture, it is essential to know the fundamentals of how a cartridge actually works. We agreed earlier that all cartridges are made to a high standard, but they can nevertheless vary considerably. This will be due to two factors: the purpose for which they have been loaded, and price.

So let us consider what a cartridge consists of.

As can be seen from the diagram, the cartridge is not a complex object. The trigger causes the firing pin to strike and indent the cap. The friction generated causes the compound to detonate a high-pressure, white-hot flame which ignites the main powder charge. This burns very rapidly, producing a large volume of hot gases which build up pressure within the cartridge. This pressure acting upon the base of the wad starts the charge up the barrel and as the gases continue to evolve it is very rapidly accelerated until it clears the muzzle at around 1200 to 1300 feet per second. This all happens in about one five-thousandth of a second.

In clay shooting competitions, virtually everyone will use a cartridge with a plastic wad. The modern one-piece plastic wad will throw much more consistent, and slightly tighter, patterns than a biodegradable fibre wad. The latter, however, may be the choice of grounds where environmental restrictions are in operation. The game shooter may also prefer a fibre wad where the slightly more open pattern is something of an advantage. Also, the right, hard-hitting pattern of a trap shooting cartridge is not recommended for the average pheasant shoot because it can result in badly shot birds which are both inedible and unsellable as a result, whereas the more open pattern from a fibre wad is ideal for this job.

The reason for the tighter patterns is that with the one-piece unit made of injection-moulded plastic, an over-powder cup seals off the gases while the shot pellets are contained in a separate cup and are therefore protected from the barrel walls as they travel out of the gun. The pellets are therefore still perfectly uniform in shape on leaving the barrel and will consequently fly straight and true. This is also where the quality of the shot comes into the equation. The harder the shot the less the distortion.

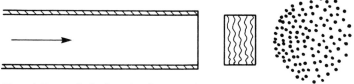

Figure i True cylinder barrel and high-quality shot gives a uniform shot string

Figure ii Choked cylinder or lower quality cartridges provide a longer shot string and hence a tighter pattern

And a perfectly symmetrical sphere will fly much truer than shot that has gone out of shape.

So, taking it to the extreme, an inexpensive fibre wad cartridge (which because of price will have cheap soft lead shot) will provide a much more open and erratic pattern due to the fact that gases seep up the side of the shot, but more importantly the shot will be fighting for space as it travels up the barrel walls and many of the round lead pellets will get distorted in the rush. The distorted pellets may well become more erratic fliers still once they have left the gun, depending on the extent of distortion. Meanwhile a top-quality competition trap cartridge with plastic wad and very hard shot will throw a perfectly predictable tight pattern. This is why when shooting at normal ranges (other than trap shooting) relatively little choke is needed.

A couple more points before we move away from the subject. Cartridges are classified as 2½, 2¾ or 3 inch. This describes the gun chamber length for which the cartridge is designed, not the actual length of the cartridge or case. A 2½-inch cartridge is for use in guns having 2½-inch chambers or longer, similarly 2¾-inch is for 2¾-inch chambers or longer, and 3-inch is for 3-inch chambers or longer. There are still one or two old side-by-sides with 2-inch chambers, but 2-inch cartridges are not easy to get hold of nowadays. The standard game cartridge for side-by-sides is 2½ inches, and the clay target shell now tends to be 2¾ inches for the modern over-under.

Your choice of shot size will also be determined by the type of target at which you are shooting. For game shooting it is best to use No. 6 or 7, for duck 5 or 6, for geese 1 or 3 and for clays 7, 8 or 9 (depending on the range and presentation of target – more about this in the respective chapters on the clay disciplines).

I would always suggest that people bear in mind that a shotgun has a maximum range of 40 yards – any further than that and it ceases to be effective with any predictability. On the other hand, you should remember that shot travels in the order of 300 to 350 yards, so you must think in terms of a 350-yard safety zone. This is also the distance recommended by the CPSA for shoot organizers.

Finally, there is generally no need to think of using a very high-velocity cartridge. Used by some top shooters, their speeds of between 1150 and 1200 feet per second are invariably hard on the shoulder. The price you pay for the extra speed isn't worth it. The faster the cartridge, the greater the recoil – there really is no way round it. Better to go for a good-quality cartridge of 1100 to 1120 fps which throws consistent patterns and can be shot in comfort. Recoil not only causes an aching shoulder and neck, it can wear you down, induce a flinch or give you a headache – all three of which have a harmful effect on your performance. This often makes me think of my motor racing days. The flashy fast drivers who screeched through the corners were seldom the ones who were first past the winning post. The smooth drivers who took least out of themselves and their cars were always much more likely to succeed.

Most cartridges are loaded with lead shot, though you will see some top trap shooters using nickel loads – these are not nickel in fact, but lead pellets coated with nickel.

Due to environmental restrictions there are now some places around the world, notably in wildfowling areas, where steel shot is compulsory. This is not a satisfactory lead substitute and can only be used on chromed-barrel guns – steel shot would ruin a Purdey barrel, for instance. There is much work to be done in finding a suitable lead alternative. Eley have recently announced a tungsten/polymer compound shot which sounds very promising, though it is too expensive for general use at present and produced in limited shot sizes. It may well, however, fit the bill for those on wildfowling expeditions who do not expect to make big bags. And no doubt if it proves satisfactory it offers the basis for further development.

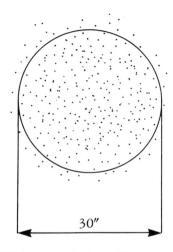

With a true cylinder and low-quality shot the pellets will spread – at 20 yards, 80% will fall within a 30-inch pattern

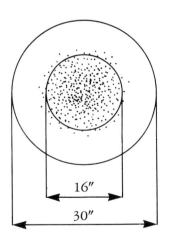

With full choke and high-quality shot the pattern will be tighter

CHOKE

A standard one-ounce load of 7-shot will have 340 pellets and in trap the object of the exercise is to have as many as possible of the pellets within a 30-inch circle at the point you expect to be hitting the target.

The choke in the muzzle of your gun will help you achieve this. For close-range targets you will need little choke but for longer range it may well be advisable to maybe have ½ choke. Therefore, most fixed-choke over-under guns are nowadays sold with ¼ in the bottom barrel and ½ in the top. This is estimated on the assumption that the first shot will be at the nearest bird and the second at a bird which is further away – either the second of a pair or, if the first barrel is a 'miss', then a little more choke is available for the second. This principle works for walking-up game or going-away clay targets, but is not at all suitable for driven pheasants whether for game shooting or a sporting clay discipline. There is, however, a barrel-select catch on most guns so that in sporting clay shooting you can easily change the sequence.

In trap shooting, the target at its launching point is 16 yards from the gun, so clearly the first shot will be some distance and the second at extreme range. Consequently, trap shooting guns tend to be choked ¾ full. This is also necessary because the target is always edge-on to the gun, that is, the clay flies flat through the air – a tight pattern will be crucial to the breaking of the clay.

If you look at the diagrams on the left, the effect of using a choke is illustrated at a range of 20 yards. A true cylinder at a greater distance of 40 yards, the maximum effective distance for clay shooting, will only place 40 per cent of the pellets in a 30-inch pattern, whereas a full choke achieves 70 per cent. A half choke achieves 60 per cent, so this is perhaps a good second barrel for the sporting clay shooter. For most shooting circumstances, ¼/¼ is probably the most adequate setting.

SHOT STRING

Another factor to be taken into account is the shot string; that is, the column of shot as it travels through the air.

Bearing in mind that there may be 350 pellets in a pattern, the shot string can stretch to around 12 to 15 feet. However, as the column is travelling faster than the speed of sound, it can in practical terms never compensate for inaccurate shooting. But psychologically it can help when shooting crossing targets – you really needn't worry about excessive forward allowance because the target might fly into the tail end of the shot column!

Note that the shot column is marginally longer on more open chokes than tighter ones, where the pattern tends to be more concentrated.

The shot from a gun travels through the air in a column

4 Getting Started

For most people the later they start any sport the more frustration it causes. I'm not sure that this is absolutely true. Shooting, for example, is a little different. While 12 years is an ideal age to start, this is a sport at which novices of any age can progress quickly. However, it has to be done with professional supervision. In fact I don't care what the sport or skill is: parents or friends are usually unsuitable for passing on important information with regard to the serious business of learning. I was perhaps lucky, but in general terms I have personally found that professional educators are considerably more successful at not only passing on information, but also ensuring that pupils enjoy the experience. Whether learning to drive a car, swing a golf club, play tennis, or shoot, well-intended parental advice can on many occasions do little to enhance either knowledge or enthusiasm for the particular endeavour.

So, for me, the first priority in the case of shooting is to go to a shooting school. However, don't go to the first one that you see. Look around. For a youngster, find an instructor who is well known for being particularly good with young people. There are, on the other hand, many instructors who are well suited to passing on their skill to more mature students, yet they may not be particularly good communicators to the young. It takes a very different skill and, after all, this is merely an introduction to the sport. There is a need to establish a solid understanding of the most basic 'do's and don'ts', to understand gun handling, and, most importantly, to drive home fully the elements of safety. If the basic rudiments are passed on successfully and are, therefore, fully absorbed, the rest will follow without too much difficulty.

And remember that just because Father is a brilliant shot it does not automatically follow that he will be a good purveyor of knowledge. An example of how strongly I feel about this is that although I won three World Championships driving racing cars I chose to send both of my sons to

We cater for all levels of instruction – including beginners of all ages

the British School of Motoring to be taught to drive in preparation for their driving tests. I am sure that I did the right thing, because although I am able to teach the more advanced techniques of car control and driving, I certainly could not guarantee success with a beginner, particularly a member of my own family.

Shooting instruction for the young beginner should start at a shooting school because the impatience of youth usually precludes long classroom sessions before the gun is put into the hands of the pupil. This is what the enthusiasm is all about. When that first experience has been enjoyed, full information can then be passed on about the basic requirements of stance, poise, movement and general technique. None of these skills, as in any sport, can be picked up overnight, and therefore a course of lessons should be undertaken. Not just one or two.

The same instructor should be used through the complete course, provided you are satisfied that the right person has been selected in the first place. This gives the tutor and the pupil the opportunity to build a relationship of understanding and allows the instructor continuity in controlling the progress with the authority required.

As far as the gun is concerned, I believe that you have to put the horse before the cart. That is to say, do not purchase the gun, especially for a young person (boy or girl), prior to being introduced to the sport. At the very young age of 12 or so, the best choice of gun for those first shots is a ·410 – most good shooting schools will have one available. It can be disastrous for a young person to be affected badly by recoil and put off the sport unnecessarily. The ·410 is light, and produces a bang, but without the kick of a 20- or 12-bore. One of the principal concerns of the instructor during the introductory stage is avoiding the flinching that can occur with a shooter using a gun. Any beginner is apprehensive about the noise and recoil and may instinctively flinch, but there are ways of greatly reducing this.

At this early stage there will be plenty of excitement in simply having the opportunity of shooting without necessarily owing a gun. That can come later when the correct dimensions, weight and calibre can be chosen. A ·410 will break almost every clay pigeon that can be thrown, and during the early lessons the targets are not too demanding in terms of speed or distance.

Also it is valuable for a novice to be shown the power of the forces within the capacity of a gun. A variety of demonstrations can be arranged to create a most spectacular effect. It has to be graphic, and in my opinion frightening, so that the implications of error or carelessness are ingrained into the pupil's mind once and for all. I also believe that it is no bad thing for any shooter to be reminded by a demonstration of the damage that can be inflicted by a shotgun. One shot into the muddy ground or at a water-melon usually gets the message across.

After a beginner has gone through his or her first series of shooting school lessons and become proficient I always think that it is good for them to be taken out on a day's shooting in the field in the company of a gamekeeper. The novice should be allowed to carry his gun but without cartridges. The spontaneous reaction of most people to a bird flying over them or being flushed in close proximity contradicts everything that they have been told in the controlled conditions of the shooting school environment. Suddenly the gun goes up to address the target swinging through a line of shooters in a manner that can put many people at risk. The new shooter has to learn another set of 'do's and don'ts', has to see how others behave and be told by an experienced keeper what can and cannot be shot at.

Such days will be invaluable and equip the new shooter with a discipline which will serve him well throughout his shooting life. He will learn the most comfortable way to carry a gun in a manner safe to all concerned, how to manage a cartridge bag or cartridge belt, how to walk over rough ground carrying a gun without risk of stumbling or falling, whilst still being able to pay attention to what might be occurring in the air. There is a correct way to cross a fence or a gate, to handle a gun in the presence of others, and to deal with and carry game.

As in most activities in life, good manners and etiquette are important. A gamekeeper can be tremendously valuable in passing on such gems of information that many fathers, uncles or other family members simply either wouldn't know or wouldn't have thought of. The novice or young shot learns more about the countryside, the environment, and the innumerable species of fowl and plants on a day in the field and all this can provide a wonderful base of knowledge that will be invaluable. Remember, the gamekeeper is the real professional.

Such outings are then best followed by more shooting school experience, and then after further training the beginner might be given the opportunity of shooting in the field. He will still be under the direction of a keeper and must be with him at all times. Also the beginner will have only one cartridge in his gun. This should not take place, however, until the pupil is well enough groomed and prepared, nor at too tender an age. When the time is right the young shooter should be supervised by adults he is familiar with and who are close enough at hand to give confidence and at the same time lend an air of authority. It is extremely uncomfortable to be shooting with others when you are concerned about their safety and experience.

In shooting, where much takes place in the winter months, wearing the correct clothes is important. If one is going to stand out in the cold and very often wet fields, the best advice is to be sure of a bit of warmth and comfort. I find that if my feet and hands are warm the rest of my body will hold up. Moreover, poor form and dangerous shooting can result from being very cold – it is virtually impossible to be fluid in movement and there is always a danger of pulling the trigger involuntarily when you're frozen.

Specialized wear is hardly necessary, however, at this stage. I always feel that as a parent who has gone through the expensive experience of providing clothing for growing children, it makes sense to buy clothes with as many uses and applications as possible. Most young folk need to have wellington boots. If you buy the right green wellies they will probably be worn much more enthusiastically. In the past wellie-boots have been well known for producing cold feet, but the better makers today, such as Gates, have overcome many of the old problems by using good insulation. Warm, dry feet go a long way to making even the coldest day acceptable or even comfortable. A heavy pair of socks or little thermal bootees worn inside the wellies can also make all the difference whilst dispensing with the risk of a chill or a heavy cold.

Waterproof trousers are also vital and have three beneficial qualities: they keep the rain out; they keep the wind out; and because of the extra layer, they create a thermal effect and so keep the heat in.

For the upper half of the body, again, whether it's autumn, winter or early spring, there may well be a lot of standing about in the cold and so warm clothes are needed. A good old-fashioned vest is a good way to start because in shooting too much clothing will restrict movement and the feel of the gun to the shoulder. Also it is best not to wear anything close-fitting because tightness restricts movement. Therefore on shirts and sweaters sleeves have to be comfortable at the armpit to allow the gun to be raised to the shoulder with ease. The left arm (if the shooter is right-handed) has to be able to stretch to the fore-end of the gun, and the right arm has to be able to bend comfortably to open up the shoulder for the stock and of course to use the trigger. So a shirt that has sleeves that aren't too generous in their length or width would be wrong. The same applies to the fitting around the body, shoulders, cuffs and neck. With plenty of space available you will be more comfortable and the clothes will last longer.

A turtle-neck sweater is also a good idea because it gives warmth to the neck without being too bulky. A V-neck sweater can even be worn over it, which both looks good and is comfortable. It is advisable to have some protection for the neck, and towelling scarves or cravats are very useful in wet weather. Once water trickles down your neck, your day is never quite the same!

Finally, because of the elements there is nothing better for outdoor country activities than a Barbour-type jacket. They are waterproof, windproof and generally the pockets are in all the right places. They are multi-purpose and seldom look out of place.

I also always encourage shooters to wear a hat. I choose a flat cap while others opt for a trilby, deerstalker or whatever is their preference. Again it's not just a question of dealing with the elements of rain and cold: it also serves a useful purpose, especially when clay pigeon shooting where it will protect the head from possible attack from broken clays! And the right headgear looks good too – and if you look the part you feel good, which in turn helps your confidence. So, dress really can have a major contributory effect towards the success of an individual's performance.

When I was at the height of my clay pigeon shooting career the way I dressed was part of a ritual and I always wore the same clothes. This was not because I was superstitious but so that on every occasion I wore exactly the same weight of clothes with the same thickness. Any alteration, of course, would have affected the length of the stock of my gun and its fit.

I used to wear the same long-sleeved light blue shirt and my special collarless jacket. I had the jacket made (yes, even in those days!) by a tailor in Scotland with no lapels so that there was nothing to get in the way of the stock as I mounted the gun. The sleeves and shoulders were the right length and size so that the jacket was neither uncomfortable nor awkward when I stretched to raise the

Knickerbockers, or breeks, are comfortable, and really look the part!

gun to my shoulder. The pockets were stitched in specific positions and could carry a certain amount of cartridges. This served two purposes: firstly, it meant that I wasn't always searching for a box of cartridges whilst actually shooting, and secondly the weight of the cartridges in my pocket held down the jacket so that there weren't any creases or wrinkles when I got the gun up to my shoulder.

All of those things made a big difference. I even wore

There are any number of accessories for 'the shooter who has everything' – such as this Spanish cartridge pouch

the same hat every time I shot, and because my eyes have always been sensitive to light mine was an American skipped cap that protected me from overhead light. By wearing the same garments my gun felt more comfortable each time I used it and therefore was always compatible in every way with my body. In most instances I would have preferred to have got soaking wet than to have changed from my regular shooting 'outfit'.

For general shooting Barbours are very good jackets in all these respects. It is easy with a Barbour to mount the gun in the same place every time – the gun doesn't catch on the material and there are no pockets or lapels in the way.

At my shooting school I mostly wear a tweed plus-two shooting suit, which I find extremely comfortable. The jacket itself has lapels but is cut in a manner that allows me to address the gun to my shoulder without any inconvenience. I wear knickerbockers because, apart from being comfortable, I think they really look the part, which I feel is very important. For this reason I am not a great believer in people wearing shooting vests that are covered in badges. Vests are fine in themselves, particularly for clay shooting, but the patches just don't look right, in my opinion, at sporting clay shoots.

Our instructors at the shooting school all wear knickerbockers, and collar and tie. Depending on the weather they will wear a Barbour, shooting jacket or vest. We are in the service industry at Gleneagles and so we must present ourselves in a manner appropriate for the hotel and our clients. We must be neat, tidy and clean at all times. But one of the things I like about sporting clay shooting is that it is not as highly geared at skeet or trap – it is a little more rural and relaxed. That is definitely something which I prefer.

Shooting is a sport which lends itself so well to clothes and colours which blend in with the environment, particularly greens and browns. A smart casual outfit, maybe with a bright sweater, has the right look for our sport.

Many people wear glasses for shooting purely for protective purposes, which is a good idea. Some also have coloured lenses which enhance vision in certain light. When I go partridge shooting in Spain it's almost essential for all shooters to wear protective eyewear. Some of the birds fly fast and low and in the excitement of the moment people sometimes shoot without a thought for the other guns. Sometimes a ricochet can result in a pellet hitting someone in the eye.

I have no hesitation in wearing glasses there. They have shatterproof lenses and protective sides against the possibility of a shot coming from a side angle. Here we also have alternative lenses available for different types of light, and it surprises me that these glasses are not worn more often on the grouse moors where birds can also be difficult to pick out against the heather in certain light conditions.

The biggest problem with wearing any kind of eyewear occurs when it rains. This is both distracting and annoying, and there is little that you can do about it. I very much sympathise with those who have to wear glasses on such days.

There is a list of garments that are essential in shooting: a Barbour (or something similar), wellingtons, a shooting vest (for clays) and a good strong pair of leather shoes. Some items, however, are a matter of preference while others come with experience. For example, some clay shooters prefer to wear sports trainers, because they do not need protective footwear but instead look for something which is light, comfortable and flexible and keeps them in contact with mother earth. Also leather shooting gloves can cost a lot of money and I think that for beginners they are unnecessary. A good pair of woolly gloves does a first-class job. They can be bought inexpensively and usually have an overlapping knit arrangement that can be used to keep the fingers warm when not shooting.

All of the items mentioned above can be used in everyday life without being so specialized that they look out of place, and at the same time the look will appeal to any young person.

As time goes by, a tweed shooting suit might appear on the shopping list but this can most definitely wait. What cannot wait, however, are shooting lessons. They represent a necessary investment for the future, particularly because we are dealing with a gun. In most sports one or two mistakes are part of the learning process. With a gun that is not so. It is imperative that the enormous responsibility is ingrained in the minds of all young shooters.

I think that, as a sport, shooting is highly character building for young people and this is why I chose to introduce both of my sons to it at an early age, to give them the feeling that they had to be responsible for their own actions and to give them something they could take pride in. They soon began to understand the importance of looking after their guns and of personally cleaning and caring for them. The gun is to be respected and its use has to be controlled with a presence of mind and a sense of discipline like no other piece of sporting equipment. The manner in which it is kept, carried and used almost defines the person. You can tell a lot about an individual by the way he or she behaves with a gun.

All young people have to be taught how to be responsible and respectful. There are so many different ways of doing this and I believe shooting is a wonderful way to assist in the process of growing up and learning the ways of life in a most positive fashion. Shooting lessons can be given as birthday or Christmas presents, or as rewards for success and the experience will go much further than just the act of learning to shoot. It can be a philosophical and psychological introduction to responsible living.

Sixty per cent of the people who go through our shooting school at Gleneagles have never lifted a gun before. Forty per cent of the total are women and shooting is one of those rare activities in sport where women can do equally as well as men in any category. It has, in the past, been a very chauvinistic activity and still to this day there are far too few lady shooters involved in game shooting. In equestrian events many of the best cross-country riders are ladies and often in open events they are outright winners.

Shooting offers the same opportunity. Women can shoot with the same guns and have equally good eyesight – and there is no penalty with respect to the strength of men versus women. The reflex actions and co-ordination are no different. We have a sport, therefore, that can be mastered by both sexes equally.

5   The First Lesson

Safety

Always think of the environment – at Gleneagles we insist that spent cartridges are never left lying around and we provide large bins for shooters to throw them into

When a beginner comes for their first shooting lesson at Gleneagles, we draw their attention to the fact that there are no empty cartridge cases lying around in the shooting area. I may be considered very fussy about the environment but I don't like to see the place looking either untidy or generally unpleasant to the eye, which is what multi-coloured spent shells most definitely are. It is obviously also wrong to leave any kind of rubbish lying around.

So our instructors always say to their pupils: 'By the way, you will notice that there are no empty shells lying around on the ground. Jackie has a rule that after shooting, all empty cartridges be picked up and deposited in the containers available. He doesn't like to see the environment looking cluttered in any way.' It doesn't matter where we are in the countryside, we should not spoil it for the lack of a little thought. When we introduced this rule my logic was simple enough – on completion of a tennis lesson, for instance, we wouldn't hesitate to pick up all of the balls at the net and put them in the basket so that the court is ready for the next pupil. Why should we in shooting be any different to anyone else?

When I first suggested the idea, however, it wasn't at all well accepted. Everybody, and I mean everybody, said they couldn't see it happening because the kind of people who come to stay at a five-star hotel such as Gleneagles are not without money and are used to being looked after. They are not going to want to pick up their own cartridges, I was told. Yet nobody to my knowledge has refused to do it.

You set a standard and people will maintain it. It is very interesting when we have our celebrity events that even members of the Royal Family don't hesitate to collect their spent shells – they see how clean and tidy the place looks and they don't want to leave it less tidy than when they arrived. I think that it is just a question nowadays of good manners and trying to keep the place as clean and tidy as we can.

This, I feel, is a very important part of the first lesson. Attention to detail is crucially important to success in any given aspect of life. To introduce a degree of order to what you are doing disciplines the mind into giving your best. It also establishes good habits for the novice shooter from the outset.

When it comes to actually shooting, the first priority without any question is safety. Good gun manners and correct gun handling say a great deal about a person. If you see someone who handles a gun sweetly and with some delicacy you are invariably looking at someone who with the appropriate quality of education will be able to shoot well. People who handle guns like pickaxes generally don't tend to be safe and don't shoot so well either.

Safety in sport has always been important to me – at Gleneagles we have netting 'cages' for spectators' safety

Correct gun handling is one of the first things we teach at Gleneagles because safety is our highest priority, and we try to instil in our students good etiquette and respect for the gun from the outset

But above all else, however people handle the gun, safety must always come first. The shotgun must at all times, other than at the point of firing, be broken and unloaded – with the breech open it is possible for all to see that there are no cartridges in it. This is one of the first points we cover and emphasize in our shooting lesson – the most important thing of all is to be a safe shot.

So we show the pupil how to hold the unloaded gun to make sure that it sits nicely in the arm, with the trigger guard behind the forearms, so that it doesn't slip forward and so that it is in a comfortable position to be carried. At no time should the gun be closed while being carried – it simply isn't possible to be 100 per cent sure that it isn't loaded. Many traditional game shooters fall down on this point. They presumably consider that because they have been shooting for many years they are by instinct 'safe'. This is nonsense. They are also human and all humans are prone to error. With a shotgun, one error in a lifetime is enough to cause a fatal accident and this should never be forgotten. Shooting isn't like dominoes or tiddlywinks – guns can be very dangerous. But guns don't kill – it is people who do this, and in safe hands a gun is never dangerous. We are responsible and control the situation.

At the shooting school we have over-unders and side-by-sides because we like to be able to offer the choice. The over-under is without question the more accurate gun to shoot with but I recognize that the side-by-side is still the gun with which a lot of people feel they want to shoot. But either way, both of these guns are easily recognized as empty and safe when broken (barrels open). With a semi-automatic, however, it is not easy for someone to see whether the breech is open or closed and whether the gun may in fact be ready to fire. These guns are also much more awkward to carry around so that the barrels are always pointed at the ground, Often you see them being carried parallel with the ground, and as a consequence the muzzles might be aiming at someone's midriff (not a pleasant experience for the

This is how the gun should be carried, empty and broken with the forearm forward of the trigger guard

It is easy with an over-under or side-by-side to check whether the breach is empty

person involved). Such behaviour is bad manners as well as being dangerous, so the etiquette of shooting is a very important element in the learning process.

As I mentioned earlier, the ideal starting point for a youngster is to go out in a game or rough shooting situation with a keeper having had the striker pins removed from his gun, but in any event carrying an empty gun. The accompanying keeper or instructor can then keep an eye on him to make sure he is doing everything correctly, whether he is judging range correctly (it is wrong to shoot at out-of-range quarry) and whether he is safe in the company of other shooters. The great worry in a live bird-shooting situation is swinging the gun through the line of other guns. Training and familiarization with an empty gun is a tremendous help.

There was a great rush of yuppies who took up the sport during the years of the booming stock-market, when endless takeovers and buyouts brought untold sums of money to many young people. Shooting was the socially acceptable thing to do and many estates had never seen anything like it. There were more fresh new shooters coming into shooting (not all young, I must add) and two-gun shoots than I had seen in my lifetime. Many of these people were not ready to shoot game with one gun, let alone two – they hadn't been given the right education, in fact in many instances no education at all. I wouldn't suggest that there was an outbreak of fatal shooting accidents, but there certainly were plenty of narrow escapes and I know of many people who shot in such company and were truly frightened by what took place.

The simple answer is to learn the slow way. You cannot have a quick lesson in shooting – it has to be repetitive and, if you intend doing any game shooting at all, it also has to be in the field as well as on clay pigeons. One must be totally at ease in a game-shooting situation. The mixture of adrenaline and surprise can have unfortunate consequences for an inexperienced shot – a rush of blood to the head and all mental discipline is gone. And it can also happen with an old experienced shot on a grouse moor just as easily as a newcomer. So always think before pulling a trigger and ask yourself: 'Is it safe?'

Your first lesson at a shooting school will, therefore, concentrate on gun etiquette and how to behave with a gun. There are aspects to shooting that simply are not present in other sports. But at the end of the day good manners in any activity are very important – in this modern, fast-travelling world we live in, manners seem to have disappeared everywhere you look, but I still believe that they can take you anywhere and hold the key in all areas of life.

Stance

After safety we can then start to look at the actual shooting of the gun. Gunfit, swing and accuracy are all important but the correct stance is essential for good shooting. It is how we stand which will dictate how well we shoot. Take a look at any excellent shot and carefully observe his stance. He will look composed, elegant, in control. Then look at someone who finds it a bit of a struggle. His stance will be awkward, his body probably twisted and generally totally ill at ease.

Stance is where everything begins. If your feet are not right no matter what the sport, be it tennis, golf, darts, snooker or shooting, then you simply won't perform. The whole foundation of what you are attempting to do bases itself on where and how you are in contact with mother earth.

You will need a stance which is relaxed but gives you total control. I tell my pupils that they should imagine that they are on the deck of a yacht in rough water. I ask them where they would put their feet. The answer is that their legs would be slightly splayed, and that they would put slightly more weight on the left leg (for the right-hander), which in turn would be slightly forward of the right leg in order to take the pitch of the yacht with the oncoming waves. And the knees would be bent very slightly, and your body generally would be flexible to lean into the forward motion of the yacht. If you hit a roller you need to be able to flex your knees to accommodate the movement. If at the same time the yacht were to roll as well as pitch, your legs being slightly apart and your feet being splayed would still give you a sure-footed stance to accommodate the roll as well as the pitch while your weight distribution leaning forward would still be in the direction of travel.

So when shooting, by leaning forward, and perhaps sticking your bottom out very slightly, you are pushing against the recoil that you are about to experience – or,

Feet should be slightly splayed, with the knees fractionally bent and more of the weight on the left foot

The correct stance is essential for good shooting

more accurately, that you would *otherwise* have experienced. With the correct stance recoil is not nearly as hard, and is more comfortably absorbed by your body.

Too many people shoot with an arched back or with too much weight on their right foot. This is an extremely uncomfortable-looking stance which is more like the rifle position of shooting than shotgun.

With a shotgun, however, it doesn't matter whether you are shooting at clay pigeons or live quarry, you have to be able to reach that target easily and quickly, and this requires the shooter to swing the gun. You need to be flexible. It is not an abrupt movement. There should be no hint of stiffness in any aspect of shotgun shooting – there has to be flow because, just as in golf, there has to be a follow through in the swing. Most people who miss do so because they stop the movement of the gun and then snatch at the target. When you see great golfers like Greg Norman and Nick Faldo swing a golf club you will notice that throughout the entire movement their swing has the kind of fluidity that we hackers can only dream about. But it's that smooth swing that gives them the distance – style means everything. Similarly if you watch the finest shots in the world you see an elegant swing and a wonderful

This is the incorrect stance – I'm leaning back, off-balance and my body will absorb none of the recoil

This stance is also incorrect – I'm actually in a rifle stance, with my hands too close together and my body inflexible and awkward. Look for a comfortable stance

follow through. Never the rapid poking and hoping, the hallmark of less successful competitors or game shots.

Without style and fluidity of movement it will still be possible to shoot well from time to time but never with any consistency. And high scores at clay pigeon shooting will be impossible. So this whole business of fluidity, that nice relaxed stance and swing, has a great deal to do with the kind of competence, accuracy and consistency that we are looking for.

Of course it's difficult to achieve all of this to begin with. It has taken me years to learn, but starting off the correct way can certainly cut years off corrective education at a later point in your shooting career. If the basics are mastered properly then more advanced techniques will be picked up much more easily. Once the pupil has adopted the correct stance and good weight distribution he can then take a gun in his hands in the knowledge that he will be able to make the most of his instruction.

Holding the Gun

When using an over-under, the left hand holds the fore-end under the barrels. I use my forefinger to point, as if I were pointing at the object which I am going to be shooting at. In fact, you may find that this happens quite naturally and that your forefinger will automatically take up a pointing position on the fore-end.

The grip should be at the length that is comfortable to you. This is unlike holding a rifle where the left hand should be close to the body so that the elbow leans against the body to steady the shooter. The leading arm is held much straighter on a shotgun.

The right hand (and in all instances I am referring to right-handed shooters) should be in control of the stock and neatly and firmly wrapped around the pistol grip on

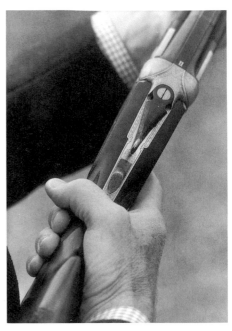

Top left: The left hand's grip is at the fore-end under the barrels, with the forefinger pointing at the target
Above: The right hand's grip looks neat and is firmly in control of the stock
Left: The first finger only holds the trigger when it is about to pull it – and the thumb is away from the safety catch

over-unders or simply the neck of the stock with straight-stocked side-by-sides. Your first finger should comfortably be able to reach and pull the trigger, but do not hold it on the trigger other than when shooting. Your thumb meanwhile should be in a comfortable reach position for the safety-catch, but placed immediately behind it when firing. This is necessary because otherwise the recoil may cause the catch to hit the end of your thumb quite sharply. Simply wrap it around the neck of the stock. We tend to use single-trigger guns at

Gleneagles which are much simpler to learn on than double triggers.

When holding the gun, only a lightish grip is needed but enough for you to be in control. You will also balance the gun evenly between the two hands.

By far the most common mistake made when novices first hold a gun is that they invariably point the muzzles downwards. One of the first things I tell a pupil is that the point of the gun must be higher than the stock before you start to lift it to your shoulder. Most beginners address the stock to their shoulder and then bring their left hand up and the barrels into line. This looks extremely awkward and is a very real handicap to successful shooting. The point, or muzzle, of the barrels should be in a position slightly above your head before the stock is raised. You will then pick up the target before you even mount the gun.

INTO THE SHOULDER

The point where the stock meets the shoulder is extremely important to the whole exercise because if the stock is not in the correct position several untoward things can happen. First of all, the recoil will be more painful. Secondly, if the butt is not high enough in the shoulder, your eyes will not be in a position to be able to look down the barrels correctly.

So where does the stock settle? As described in an earlier chapter on buying guns, for the right-hander, take your left hand and feel across your chest to your right shoulder. The outside of your shoulder is fairly meaty and muscular, but the bony area of your shoulder is clearly not the right place for you to address the stock of the gun, for it would cause considerable discomfort from the recoil.

As you move your hand in from the shoulder, however, you will find a more fleshy recessed area just below your collar-bone. If you lift your elbow you will find that this area opens up perfectly to accommodate the butt of a

This is what I call the 'sweet spot', the fleshy pocket of your shoulder where the gun should be mounted every time

Practise finding the right spot in
your shoulder

stock. Put your left fist or the edge of your left hand in
there and feel it. Then place your stock against it. Try it a
few times so that you know where the stock must be. Be
careful to avoid the collar-bone because recoil here will be
very painful.

THE HEAD

Having found the position of the stock to your shoulder you then have to address your head to the stock to look down the barrels themselves.

The head should be placed on the stock comfortably and again you should remember your head position because when you learn to mount the gun there will be no movement of the head. You simply hold it in the correct position so that the gun just slots into place between shoulder and cheek.

Using the forefinger of your left hand, move the flesh of your right cheek up until you feel the bottom of the cheekbone. Then cup your forefinger underneath that cheekbone and press the flesh of your cheek upwards to create a cushion below the actual cheekbone. That is the position where the comb of your stock should be when addressed to the face.

If you also feel the bottom of your cheekbone right down to your chin you should find that the stock has little contact with the jaw. If it feels that the bone is pressing against the stock then there will be a possibility of damaging the blood vessels on the jawbone (as I myself did).

Move the flesh of your right cheek up until you feel the bottom of your cheekbone

Hold the stock firmly to your cheek, without it touching your jaw

MASTER EYE

After you have addressed the gun to your face you must always remember that your master eye must go down the line of the barrel and rib.

So how do you establish which is your master eye. The way that I do it is to take my right arm and point with my index finger to an object with both eyes open. I might point at the corner of a picture or the top of a flagpole. I then close my left eye and if the finger is still pointing directly at the object then I know that I have a right master eye and that I can safely shoot with both eyes open.

If you find that on closing your left eye your finger is no longer pointing directly at the object, you will know that your right is not your master eye. If you now open the left eye and close the right (while still pointing at the object), you should find that the finger is now actually in line with what you are pointing at. If so, you definitely have a left master eye, even though you are right-handed, and if you shoot with both eyes open you will constantly shoot behind right-hand birds and in front of left-hand birds. There will be tremendous inconsistency in your shooting.

Most people shoot shotguns with both eyes open

RIGHT MASTER EYE

Figure i If my finger is directly in line with my eye and the object, as it is here, I know that I have a right master eye

Figure ii Therefore I can safely shoot with both eyes open

LEFT MASTER EYE

Figure iii If my finger does not align with my eye and the object I have a left master eye

Figure iv If I shoot with both eyes open with a left master eye I will be very inconsistent

If this is the case you have one of three options: a cross-over stock; learn to shoot from your left shoulder; or shoot right-handed but with your left eye closed. I would definitely opt for the latter. A cross-over stock is bent to the point of presenting the barrels to the left eye and in my opinion is very unsightly. And I feel that it is far simpler to shoot with your left eye closed than to learn to shoot off your left shoulder.

So the master eye is a matter to be addressed at the outset, for unlike rifle shooters most people shoot shotguns with both eyes open.

At this point, after all the mental and physical preparation has been followed through, the gun can be loaded. This is the simplest of all aspects of shooting, yet there are many who fail to do it properly – and by this I mean safely. Remember that the barrels must at all times be pointed at the ground, and so it is the stock which is closed to the barrels rather than vice versa. In this way there is never any danger should the gun be fired accidentally. Also at Gleneagles we always insist upon pupils wearing some form of hearing protection, whether it's wax, cotton wool or 'cans'.

Always load with the barrels pointing down and pull the stock up

LOADING THE GUN

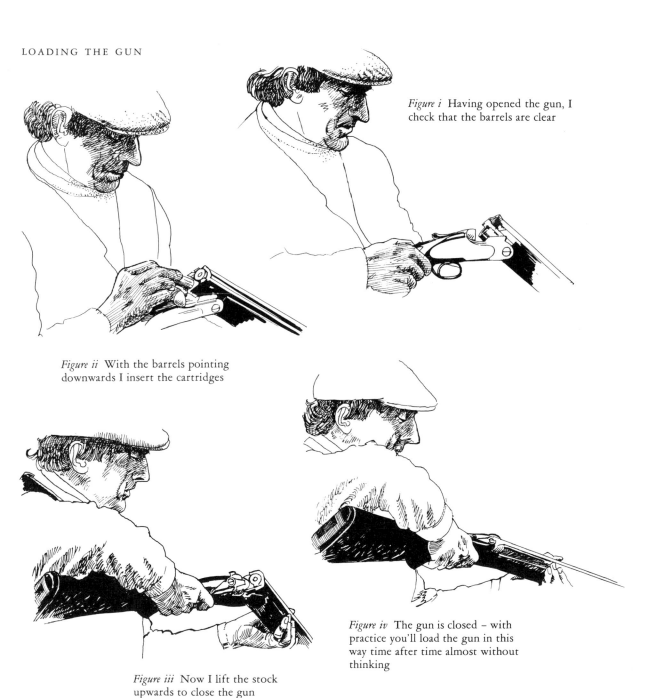

Figure i Having opened the gun, I check that the barrels are clear

Figure ii With the barrels pointing downwards I insert the cartridges

Figure iii Now I lift the stock upwards to close the gun

Figure iv The gun is closed – with practice you'll load the gun in this way time after time almost without thinking

LOCKING IN TO THE GUN

The greatest fault of all shooters, both novices and the experienced, is not keeping the head still as the shot is being taken. Once you put your gun to your shoulder and the cheek is in position on the comb of the stock, then your head should stay firmly in that position until the shots are completed.

What invariably happens is that just prior to the shot being taken the head lifts slightly to make sure of the target, and if this doesn't happen on the first shot it happens immediately afterwards as people lift their heads to see if the target has been broken. This obviously alters the sight picture and as a result innumerable targets are missed behind and over the top.

It's a bit like a golfer taking his eye off the ball – seldom will he hit it solidly and sometimes he will miss it altogether. Also with the cricketer who turns his head to where he intends hitting the ball before the stroke is actually made. And the snooker player who lifts his head from the cue just as he takes his shot. The fluency and accuracy go clean out of the window.

So you have to keep your head firmly on the stock and in the same place throughout the complete process of taking a shot. To try to get people to think about this I say to them that they should imagine that some glue is on the side of the gun stock. Once it is in position and the head is on the stock, they cannot lift their head to see if they have hit the target without pulling all that lovely skin off their cheek! Not very pleasant, but if you think in terms of something like that happening, it may help you remember the importance of keeping your head still throughout.

Think of it in another way. Picture yourself addressing an audience with a microphone in a big wide room. The good entertainer that you see on television or a live show holds that microphone so that it literally follows his mouth no matter who he speaks to, whether it's someone down in

Note how I mount the gun without moving my head

the stalls, in the circle or the left or right wing. The micro-phone never moves away from the mouth – he knows that he wouldn't be heard if it were otherwise.

It is exactly the same with the shooter. The head and eye must be constantly in the same place in relation to the shot-gun and its barrel. The eye is what makes the difference between hitting and missing the target, so you must have that eye running down the rib of the gun with the bead at the end addressing the target. Without that solid position you are not going to shoot consistently, and maybe not connect with very much at all.

If in one lesson you can fully absorb the importance of that you will have gone a long way to becoming a com-petent shot. It's a very important lesson to learn.

Again, the head remains still as the gun is
raised into the target area

The One-hour Lesson

It is extremely difficult to conduct a fully comprehensive lesson in one hour. At Gleneagles in that first one-hour lesson we only introduce people to the sport. We have most people killing five or six out of ten on the grouse butt before the lesson is finished, and for any man or woman, regardless of age, that can be a very satisfying experience. But we stress that pupils should not assume that they are fully educated. It is all too easy to jump to the conclusion having broken a few clays that perfecting their skills is just a matter of time. I am afraid life isn't like that.

Inevitably one of the frustrations for our instructors is that many of our clients come to stay at the hotel for a maximum of one, two or three days, and perhaps can shoot for only one hour on one day. They are excited and want to do it well. They want to tell everyone about their lesson at the Jackie Stewart Shooting School at Gleneagles and will be asked: 'What did they teach you?' Hopefully they'll say that we taught them the fundamentals of good shooting and that they had the thrill of breaking targets.

We also point out that this lesson is just the beginning of the education process and that every pupil should try to run through a course or series of lessons. There are many good shooting schools around the country and many good instructors. Don't make the mistake of thinking that you can do it as a self-taught exercise – you can probably get away with your errors, but for the average person it will take good instruction and years of experience to reach a decent level of consistency.

Again I must cite the example of sending my own sons to the British School of Motoring to learn how to drive before taking their driving tests – and I have won the World Formula One Motor Racing Championship three times. I am not a professional educator of driving so I sent my sons to the real professionals. The same applies to shooting, as in any sport.

We have over 12,500 people per year through our shooting school at Gleneagles. That means that each of our instructors is faced every day of the week, every week of the year, with an endless variety of tutorial challenges. Through an enormous number of hours of accumulated knowledge and experience they know how to pass on information in a positive fashion, and how to achieve results. They know how to get the new shooter to understand clearly the rudiments of the sport.

In this respect women tend to be much better learners than men. For some reason men have this misconstrued idea that they really should have lived in a different time and then they would have been Wyatt Earp or at least riding shotgun on a stagecoach. Men are under the misapprehension that they will be able to shoot by instinct, and they also have this element of bravado continually getting in the way. Women and youngsters, however, listen more carefully and are far more receptive to instruction – their progress is consequently much more rapid.

On their first shooting day I often start a novice off with the gun mounted in their shoulder rather than making them mount and shoot in one short lesson. Depending on the pupil, I may continue to let them shoot with the gun mounted for the next couple of lessons or so.

I believe it is far better for a beginner to walk before he runs and so we go through the simplest exercise to begin with. The ideal target for this first lesson is the driven grouse – an incoming target of very modest height. We find that most people can adapt to that target more comfortably than any of the others. The purpose of this is to provide knowledge and encouragement – to kill a few targets is wonderful for the pupil in both respects. The pupil enjoys the thrill of breaking the clay, gets an insight as to how it's done (which is very difficult if they are missing) and gains confidence in the process.

There is no point whatsoever in starting on a difficult target.

Taking the Target

You will notice that I have spoken at length about the preliminaries and you may by now be asking yourself, 'What about actually shooting? What's the trick?'

The 'trick' is to get all the preparation right. A gun that suits you, a stance with a nice even weight distribution, and the correct grip and mounting to your shoulder. Once you get all of these things right then all you need is a little courage! If your approach work is good then it will pay dividends because it accounts for 90 per cent of the process of breaking a target. The other 10 per cent is where you have to be brave enough to pull the trigger.

There is an optimum point at which the target should be taken. The drawback with learner shooters (and many others too) is that they tend to wait too long. They want to make sure of the shot and as a result miss that optimum moment, not to mention the target! Let me explain.

There are three principal styles of shooting: orthodox, Churchill and maintained lead. The orthodox style is the one favoured by most, and the method recommended by the Clay Pigeon Shooting Association. It is the simplest and, I believe, the most natural to learn. I shoot by this method and we instruct it at Gleneagles. It is based on the principle of mounting just behind the target, then finding its line and speed before accelerating the swing through to a given point and firing the gun.

The Churchill style is named after Robert Churchill who pioneered this particular method in conjunction with his 25-inch Churchill gun. He was a wonderful shot who made his system work and sold a lot of guns in the process. But my belief is that with less naturally co-ordinated people it can prove very erratic. With this method you pull the trigger as the gun hits the shoulder, relying on the mount, swing and 'natural co-ordination' to look after any necessary forward allowance.

Maintained lead is exactly what it says. Bearing in mind

that, for any type of shooting, the cartridge pattern needs to be placed where the target will be (rather than where it was), maintained-lead shooters hold the gun at a predetermined point in front of the target. American skeet shooters very often track the target in front, thus maintaining a lead throughout. Another version of maintained lead is described by Britain's John Bidwell, a former World Champion, as Move Shoot Mount. He mounts in front of the target to a predetermined point and shoots on mounting.

Both the Churchill and maintained lead have an element of interception about them, and this is sometimes referred to as another style in itself.

All styles of shooting have their advocates. My own belief is that the basic art of mounting on to a target, tracking and swinging through is the one that is best mastered first. After this it may be possible to experiment and use other styles for different shots – indeed some of the very top sporting shooters do just this. A beginner, though, will want to learn to hit targets in the simplest and most effective way possible. By mastering the basic essentials of clay target shooting he can build and move forward from that point. Until then he should forget the notion of methods and concentrate on what I believe is the most natural way to shoot.

As mentioned, in the first lesson we get the pupil to shoot with the gun already in his or her shoulder at the time of calling the target. Learning to mount a gun properly takes time and I feel that initial effort should be concentrated on what needs to be done to break the target.

The driven grouse, the ideal first-lesson target, is released more or less directly towards the pupil, who watches over the muzzles waiting for the optimum point. The instructor has already explained that this must be in front of the bird as it approaches, and the pupil tracks the target until the instructor says 'Now' and the pupil responds by blotting out the target from his vision with the end of the barrels and pulling the trigger, all in one movement. If not then the moment is lost and so is the clay.

The same 'gun-up' approach can be used for a going-away target. Again, if the trigger isn't squeezed at the correct moment the clay becomes much more difficult because in an instant it will be at greater distance and dropping. But taken in one sweet movement it is a good easy target to break.

It is when we come to crossing birds and high birds that pre-mounting is a disadvantage. If a bird is crossing in front of the shooter, and the gun is pre-mounted to track the clay throughout its flight, then the natural momentum will be lost. The brain is a wonderful computer and it can respond with great alacrity to information given. Therefore, on a crossing target it is better to address the given area in which the clay is likely to be broken and then wind back, holding the gun out of the shoulder but with the muzzles up so that your eyes can look over them for the source of the clay.

You call the target when you are ready – and not before. Be totally relaxed. When the clay appears you 'collect' it over the muzzles of your gun, keeping it there as you mount. Remember to keep your head still – you move the stock into the shoulder and cheek as the muzzles follow the clay across in front of you, finally mounting the gun as the clay moves into the killing area. You then track it briefly before moving in front of the target to pull the trigger.

How far in front should you move? How much forward allowance should you give? That will depend on the distance and speed of the target. But by following it all the way across its arc your eyes will have gathered a complete perspective and subconsciously your brain will calculate exactly how much in front you need to shoot. If you leave the shot too long it becomes very much more difficult. The target starts to slow and drop. Any previous momentum will be lost. So shoot at the optimum point, which is the area directly in front of you where the target can clearly be seen and is travelling at a good even speed.

Forward allowance is a matter of judgement for the shooter about which there is endless debate. Ignore the advice of other shooters because we all have different perceptions and responses. An instructor will know from watching you shoot exactly how you respond to the target and what kind of forward allowance will be needed. The average shooter will advise you but his advice will be based on what was right for him rather than what might be best for you. For example, his swing may be much faster than yours.

Don't let things get too complicated. Think in terms of the target and nothing else: you should be looking down the barrels of your gun but really your eyes are focused on the target. With the correct fit and a good mounting the gun is now merely an extension of your body, another finger with which to point. Remember that when you use your finger to point at something you do it instinctively – you don't look down your finger, but at what you are pointing at. A tennis player, golfer or cricketer looks only at the ball.

Your main problem initially is getting the right distance in front of a crossing target and keeping the gun moving when pulling the trigger. Most crossers are missed behind as a result of insufficient forward allowance. There seems to be something slightly unnatural about not shooting 'at' something – to shoot at an empty space takes confidence. Think of it in terms of throwing a ball to someone who is running across your field of vision 20 yards away from left to right. You wouldn't hesitate to throw it just in front of where they are in order for them to catch it. The principle is identical in shooting.

Also, with this type of target you may well swing in front of the target perfectly correctly when tracking it, but then stop the gun as you pull the trigger. By the time the message has gone from the brain to the finger and the trigger has been pulled, the target will have traversed the forward allowance you had created. Your shot will arrive when the clay has gone!

It's back to being brave enough to pull the trigger. As you swing in front of the target, your brain will tell you at a certain point that you should pull the trigger – don't hesitate. Take the shot in one fluid movement as the gun is moving. It all goes back to the golfer's swing, the cricketer's follow-through – keep it smooth.

Before shooting, it might help to remember that your shot has a 30-inch pattern out there (plus a shot string), so you may shoot well in front of a crosser and still hit it with the back of the pattern. Plus there is the rest of the pattern following if you haven't got it quite right. Yet despite this very few targets are missed in front.

Once you have broken two or three targets and seen how it works, it is amazing how naturally it all comes. It is just a question of building confidence, practising and getting your preparation right.

The illustration sequences in the following chapter show quite clearly what has to be done.

6 The Disciplines

Clay pigeon shooting is an unusual sport in that it has so many different guises, or disciplines as they are termed. In some ways this is part of its appeal, but in another respect it has probably held the sport back. If you say you play golf or tennis then anyone will immediately understand what you are talking about. But in clay pigeon shooting it is possible to be an international champion in up to 10 disciplines (theoretically, at least!).

The three principal ones are trap, skeet and sporting, but there are various permutations of each. Trap shooting in particular is available in a number of formats.

Trap Shooting

Trapshooting has its origins in the days of live pigeon shooting of the nineteenth century. When clay pigeons first appeared on the scene in 1880 they were thrown or released in a very similar way to that which had been adopted as the norm for live pigeons. The targets were launched from a point situated 16 or 18 yards in front of the shooter. The clay consequently was a retreating target that rose on release, levelled out and then fell as it lost its velocity. To this day the basic format remains the same, though the manner in which the disciplines are conducted has become very sophisticated.

The most popular form of trap shooting in the UK and USA is what is known in England as down-the-line and in the States as American trap. In other countries the favoured form of trap varies – in France it is automatic ball trap, while in Italy the big love is Olympic trap (indeed this is by far the most popular form of all clay pigeon shooting in Italy). As its name suggests, Olympic trap is an Olympic discipline and in my opinion it is the 'Formula One' of clay pigeon shooting – the ultimate challenge.

But let us look closer at the trap shooting options.

DOWN-THE-LINE OR AMERICAN TRAP

This is the simplest of all the trap shooting disciplines, but that is not to say that it's any easier at which to become a champion. In terms of a shooting challenge it offers straightforward targets that can be mastered quite quickly.

I learned to shoot clays myself at DTL and you quickly discover that the targets in themselves are not difficult, but that to achieve any consistent level of success great powers of concentration are needed. This in itself proved a wonderful training for me and once you have learned to sustain your concentration the benefits are enormous. The mistake which many people then make, however, is to assume that once they have achieved two or three wins, then it will not be necessary to concentrate quite so hard. This is an aspect of shooting which never changes: if you want to break a target, no matter how simple, you really have to give it your undivided attention.

So what is DTL? As you will see from the illustration, targets are shot by a squad of five shooters positioned in an arc some 16 yards behind the trap. The targets are thrown a distance of approximately 55 yards at a varying angle of 44 degrees, that is to say, 22 degrees to the left or right of centre. They will, however, fly to a constant height which is fixed by the ground owner at between 8 and 10 feet – this will vary in the UK but in the States it tends to be around 9½ feet.

The essential difference in shooting the targets in the two countries is that in the UK there is a points system by

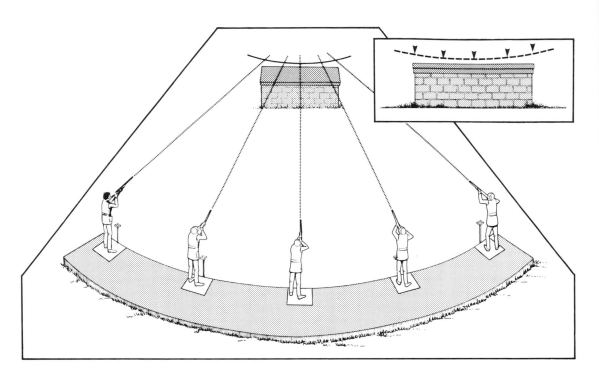

This is the down-the-line layout:
five shooters take turns at shooting
targets flying away at an angle
which varies 22° from the centre

Inset: The arrows indicate where
each shooters at each respective peg
aims before calling the target

which you get three points for a first barrel kill and two for a second. The total maximum score therefore in a 100-target competition is 100/300. In the States only one cartridge is used and the most popular form of trap is therefore known as Singles. Other than that the sequence is identical. Each shooter takes one shot at a time, and five in total on each peg before moving to the next peg, and so on, to complete a round of 25. Registered competitions are normally out of 100 targets.

With a relatively low target speed and a minimal variation in angle it would be easy to assume that this is a very simple game. As I have pointed out, however, it takes a lot of concentration to get a maximum score. The mind can easily wander. Without realizing it you may, for instance, be standing on Peg 5 and subconsciously expect that your next bird will be a slight left-hander – instead it is a sharp right-hander, you snatch at it and miss with the first barrel, then fudge your second shot. If you had hopes of winning the competition you can forget them now. A missed target and the loss of three points will be enough to put you out of most competitions. The standards are high.

As with all trap shooting, the target is called with the gun pre-mounted. According to the peg, you will hold the gun so that you are looking just above the trap house. Remember the stance for the deck of a yacht – you need to be flexible but steady.

Always be sure that you are totally ready to shoot when you call the target. Give it your undivided attention. There is often a tendency to slot into the groove of a squad – the chap before you has just shot his target and you automatically mount your gun and call 'PULL!' But you may not be ready. Never be hurried into shooting. Get yourself together. When actually shooting at the target, never be tempted to look flash and shoot very quickly; instead

Down-the-line is a relatively simple form of clay shooting, and many small clubs have a DTL layout

shoot as soon as you feel that you are ready to shoot.

With a trap gun you sit the target over the rib of your gun and as soon as you see the right picture you pull the trigger. Keep the whole thing smooth. Don't snatch, and be sure to shoot the target before it reaches the peak of its climb. If you leave your shot too long you will find that it becomes much more difficult. The target drops sharply and more targets are missed over the top than anywhere else, either through shooting too quickly and the shot flashing over the top or leaving it too late and attempting to shoot 'at' the clays when in fact they are dropping.

Your gun and ammunition   You will definitely need a trap gun for DTL or American trap. You need the extra weight and barrel length to keep on top of the situation – a light gun will whip through the target and see you missing over the top.

Trap guns tend to have slightly longer stocks but their most noticeable feature is that they shoot higher than normal guns. The stock combs are set so that you see slightly more rib than with a normal sporting or game gun. This is because all trap targets are rising and retreating and the high-shooting gun enables the shooter to keep the target in view throughout the process of the shot being taken.

Also because of the slow velocity of these birds this gun offers a very good case for 32-inch-barrel guns. The extra weight and pointability help the shooter to pick the birds out. However, I prefer the standard 30-inch trap gun.

The choke of all trap guns tends to be ¾ full. There is a good argument for more open chokes for DTL shooting, such as ½/¾, but I prefer having the confidence of tighter chokes. Nothing breeds confidence more than bringing off the kind of kills which can only be achieved with tight chokes.

There is a school of thought which suggests that the most powerful and heaviest loads permissible are the best for trap. I do not subscribe to this and I think many have been pleasantly surprised with their scores now that the 28-gram load is compulsory in registered competition.

Rather than shot load and speed, the crucial factors in ammunition (as in all disciplines) are quality and consistency. The Eley Olympic trap load, for instance, is quick though by no means the fastest cartridge available, but is consistent and smooth. A 'powerful' cartridge will induce fatigue or headache, which can have disastrous consequences on scores.

VARIATIONS

There are a number of variations of DTL or American trap. These include double rise (pairs instead of single targets) and handicap by distance, with shooters positioned according to their class at points up to 27 yards behind the trap (23 yards in the UK).

Automatic Ball Trap Often known as ABT, and very popular with many small French clubs, automatic ball trap has been called the poor man's trench (Olympic trap). This is perhaps an unfair tag but in some ways is descriptively correct.

Much more difficult than DTL but not as testing or demanding as Olympic trap, ABT utilizes only one trap but throws targets at much faster speeds and wider angles than DTL. The trap itself is 15 metres in front of the five firing points, but the trap oscillates so that in addition to throwing targets to a maximum of 45 degrees either side of centre it varies their height from one to three metres. Additionally, a round of 25 targets is shot by a squad of six shooters, taking one shot at each peg before moving to the next one. There is consequently no spare man as such for as soon as an individual has shot Peg 5 he then moves round to Peg 1, which will have been vacated by the Peg 1 shooter by the time he arrives.

ABT is certainly a very enjoyable discipline and a good

training ground for the more demanding Olympic trap and also it is the next step up from down-the-line. Combining as a test of concentration and of shooting skills, with a wide and more unpredictable range of targets, ABT represents a good test of ability.

Olympic Trap   This discipline is often known as Trench, having taken its name from the fact that the traps are installed in a trench 15 metres in front of the shooting line.

As you will see from the diagram, an Olympic trap layout is quite a complex affair. It involves the use of 15 traps, three in front of each of the five firing points. Note also that the firing points are in a straight line as opposed to an arc for DTL.

Targets are thrown to a minimum of 77 metres. The clays will rise from between one and four metres, and the traps are set at different angles ranging from straight to 45 degrees either side of the centre. They are also set in a predetermined scheme so that after the conclusion of a round

Olympic trap is the greatest challenge for the clay shooter – the Formula One of shooting

In Olympic the targets are retreating from the shooter at 90 miles per hour, at a wide variety of angles

all shooters will have received the same permutation of targets but in a different order. Some claim to be able to 'read' the scheme, but I think that such a notion is foolish, for it can lead one to wrong assumptions.

Two shots can be fired at each target. In fact many top competitors fire two barrels even if they hit a bird with the first, just to keep their hand in for the eventuality of a missed first barrel. Scoring is on kills only and competitions are out of 100 or 200 targets (the latter being two- or three-day events).

This is not a cheap discipline either to shoot or to install and Olympic trap facilities in the UK and USA are some- what rare (though American shooters invariably figure in World and European championships), so consequently it does not have as big a following as sporting or DTL.

But once you have shot Olympic trap you are spoiled for any other trap shooting. It is a test of skill and concentra- tion in which the stance, gunfit and timing must be right. With DTL you can pick out your target, but with trench you really have to harness your instincts. A smooth fluid shot, taken with the momentum of the swing, is vital.

This discipline also offers the gifted shooter the bonus

of being given the opportunity to represent his or her country in true international competition. The shooting grounds of Italy such as Montecatini, Bologna and Lonato enjoy superb facilities, and when you take part as a British team member in a World Championship at one of these venues you really get a taste of what competitive shooting is all about. Plus there is the ultimate goal of competing in the Olympics, for trench and ISU skeet are the only two disciplines that are recognized. It is a wonderful spur for the aspiring shooter and, as I mentioned earlier, not competing in the Olympics and missing qualification by one target was the major disappointment of my shooting career.

Universal Trap   This is just one step away from Olympic trap. In many respects it is the same, but instead of 15 traps there are five. The target is thrown from any one of the five, so while they tend to be slightly slower their angles can be more acute. Obviously it is less expensive to install than 15-trap, and also it is enjoyable to shoot as a second choice to Olympic.

Other forms of trap   Double Trap is a discipline which was introduced to be recognized at Olympic level. It was devised by the Europeans to stimulate interest in the sport with a short-duration competition (shot in pairs, it is inevitably concluded quicker). The 28-gram load was stipulated as mandatory and this rule subsquently spread to other disciplines. However, using two traps, one fixed and one oscillating, it was very difficult and never caught on. The rules are being revised at the time of writing.

Pro-Trap is another clay game which is being used to present the sport as more accessible to the media. Involving up to seven traps on one layout, a wide variety of targets can be shot within a relatively small area. It is, therefore, easier to film and much better from a spectator's point of view.

Sheer concentration as competitors prepare for a shoot off in the Rolex British Grand Prix, at the North Wales Shooting School

Starshot has enjoyed quite a lot of television exposure and cable TV viewing figures in the States have been good. In many ways a clay shooting equivalent of darts, with a big framework of numbered squares. The traps throw targets upwards out of the ground. Though it will probably not catch on as a participant sport, it has shown itself to be a good way of getting clay shooting on to television, where filmed under floodlights it can look quite dramatic. I actually took part in the first televised Starshot competition. There is an element of trick shooting about taking the faster shots at the bottom of the frame.

There are other forms of trap shooting, such as Euro Trap which is very similar to Pro-Trap. And another form is ZZ, where instead of clay targets a plastic propellor is used to create what is probably the closest simulation of live pigeon shooting and only 12 or 20 targets are shot in competition. There is some interest in the UK but it is only small as yet, the sport's real home at the moment probably being the Bois de Boulogne Club in Paris.

Skeet

Skeet is quite different to trap in that in this discipline it is essential to master the art of forward allowance.

As mentioned earlier, skeet is based on the 'Round the Clock' sport devised 70 years ago in Massachusetts. The seven (or eight, depending on which version) shooting positions are situated in a 21-metre-radius arc forming a semi-circle around two trap houses. The trap house to the left is elevated and situated 40 yards from the low house.

The three versions of skeet are English Skeet, ISU Skeet

English skeet layout: five shooters take turns firing from seven different positions on a semi-circle at targets released from two traps

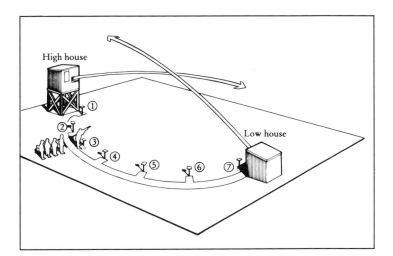

and NSSA (American) Skeet. English and NSSA have much in common. The target speeds are identical (the same as DTL and American trap). The National Skeet Shooting Association of America, however, has a slightly different shooting sequence to the English, using eight stations instead of seven. In English skeet on stations One, Two, Four, Six and Seven a single target is taken from each trap house followed by a double; on stations Three and Five only singles are released. This makes for a total of 24 birds. If all have been broken then the shooter has an option of high or low on Station Seven to complete his 25. Other-

wise he will have had a second shot at the first target
missed. NSSA skeet differs only in as much as instead of
doubles being taken on Station Four the competitor has
two singles on Station Eight. And if 'straight' at this point,
he has his option on this station.

So the two are very similar. American shooters, however, tend to prefer to shoot the discipline 'gun-up'. Scores
in the States are staggering with '400-straights' a regular
feature of the NSSA World Championships in Texas. In
the 1983 championship Wayne Mayes and Phil Murray
shot a staggering 1050 straight. These kind of scores,

Shooting at Station 1 high house on
a skeet range

therefore, put to bed any arguments against 'gun-up' for skeet. However, in the UK most skeet shooters favour gun-down, taking the targets in a similar manner to sporting. Indeed there is perhaps an element of this being the 'sporting' way of shooting skeet. In terms of overall shooting ability the individual can certainly improve his general skills far more by shooting gun-down. If he wants to concentrate on skeet and nothing else, however, then 'gun-up' may well be the answer.

International (ISU) skeet is another game altogether. As an Olympic discipline it represents the supreme challenge for the skeet shooter. For starters, the rules stipulate that when calling for the target the gun must be well out of the shoulder and the toe of the stock level with the shooter's hip bone. The targets are 20 yards faster than in other skeet, and there is a delay of up to three seconds on the target appearing after having been called. This doesn't sound very long but it can seem like an eternity.

The target sequence is as follows: Station One – high single and double; stations Two and Three – two singles and double; Station Four – two singles; stations Five and Six – two singles and double; Station Seven – double; Station Eight – two singles.

To achieve any kind of success at ISA skeet calls for devotion to the discipline, with much patience and determination. It is quite difficult to start with and many skeet shooters are so disappointed with their scores when they switch from English or NSSA skeet that they jump straight back again. Consequently, ISU skeet has only a limited following in the UK and the States. In Europe, however, it is the recognized form of skeet shooting – there is no other.

In fact ISU is a very demanding form of shooting but one from which much can be learned. Gun mounting is crucial to success at the discipline and consequently this can prove an enormous benefit to general shooting skills. International competitions are dominated by Italy, the Soviet Union and America.

Your gun and ammunition   For ISU skeet virtually all of the top international competitors use a 28-inch gun, built specifically for the purpose. In essence the difference between these guns and sporting models is slight and the tendency nowadays amongst English skeet shooters is to use a sporting gun, very often with a multi-choke.

In fact many find that the 30-inch guns are ideal for English skeet where the long barrel enables them to sustain a nice smooth swing on the long crosser of the double on Station Four. For the same reason many shooters prefer to use some choke (maybe ¼). Generally, a heavier gun of around 8 pounds tends to make skeet shooting easier.

By and large, it's best to shoot with the gun with which you feel most comfortable. I would, incidentally, warn against buying one of the old 26-inch skeet guns. These were once popular but time has proved that they are not in fact ideal for the job, quite the contrary.

When it comes to ammunition there is little choice: the rules state that 9-shot cartridges must be used. This is the perfect size for skeet so there would be no point in using anything else anyway.

Sporting

Sporting is by far the most popular discipline in Britain today. In America also it has grown rapidly during the last three or four years and it is expected to become very popular there. Already there are many excellent facilities and the sport has two associations, the USSCA and the NSCA. The USSCA is the original association and the bigger of the two, while the NSCA is linked with the NSSA. In Britain the ruling body is the Clay Pigeon Shooting Association, which governs all domestic clay pigeon shooting.

The best thing about sporting is that it is all things to all people. It can be a competitive sport for which membership of the national body is crucial, or it can be 'fun in a field' with a group of friends and a couple of traps. Because there is no formal layout the potential is considerable. The sheer variety of sporting is perhaps its greatest appeal – there are so many different targets that can be presented, and in a variety of combinations. Each shot is a challenge on its own, and a test of your ability. You don't have to be brilliant to enjoy it and it can be staged to cater for all standards.

My shooting school at Gleneagles is based on sporting targets. We have 12 different stands (or stations) simulating 12 different quarry species – crossing pigeon, driven grouse, Gleneagles pheasant, springing teal, bolting rabbit, running hare, snipe, driven partridge, king's pheasant, queen's pheasant, woodcock and duck. Each presents its

Sporting is the most popular discipline in Britain today

My feeling is that most sporting shooters prefer not to see traps and that both the targets and shooting positions should look as natural as possible

own challenge. People tend to have their own favourites but there are few who can resist the challenge of the king's pheasant, the very high-tower birds. It is an unusual experience shooting this kind of target, driven straight overhead at 100 feet, because of the enormous amount of forward allowance needed. There is a pause after your shot when nothing happens and then suddenly the clay breaks. The thrill is tremendous.

By adjusting the speed of the traps any stand can be tailored to the ability of the shooter. Alternatively, in an informal set-up the shooting position can be amended slightly to make the shooter nearer or further away from the target. We have fixed positions at Gleneagles where, with an ongoing plan for development, we put a great accent on being environmentally friendly. All of the stands and butts blend perfectly into the setting. Many of the better grounds tend to take advantage of the natural surroundings with a variety of simulated targets that look entirely natural. My feeling is that most sporting shooters prefer not to see traps and that the targets should look as natural as possible.

In a sporting competition, whether there are 25, 30, 40, 50 or 100 birds, there is always a selection of stands. On each stand there will be a given number of targets with the odd single, but mostly they will be presented in pairs: either as a pair from one trap with a double arm, or as an 'on report' pair using two different traps. Consequently, a stand such as the fur and feather may well see a bolting rabbit with the first shot followed by a crossing pigeon or teal with the second.

In all instances it is the approach work which will count towards your success. Your stance, both in terms of direction and weight distribution, your grip and mount of the gun and your taking of the target at the right point. Pulling the trigger is the final piece of the jigsaw.

In the following pages I will look at some of the stands we use at Gleneagles. I have chosen a selection which gives a good working basis on which to expand – you tend to find that each stand should be judged on its own merits but it will have certain characteristics which are similar to others.

THE GROUSE

This is the stand which we use for the first lesson. It teaches the shooter a number of fundamental points concerning stance, mounting, control and swing, but at the same time the challenge is not too great.

The shooter has to do something different than simply shoot at a target if he wishes to hit it. Remember the deck of the yacht and note my stance. I am standing upright with my legs slightly apart and feet at two o'clock. I can move my body easily without it affecting the stability of my

Figure i Remember to stand with your feet apart and your knees flexed, like the stance you might take on the deck of a rolling yacht

stance. The gun stock is out of my shoulder but the barrels are in the air. More than that, they are pointing in the direction of the source of the target – I will easily be able to pick up the clay over the muzzles when it appears.

As the target comes towards me, keeping the muzzles of the gun 'on' the clay I mount the gun. I am looking at the clay throughout, locked into it in effect – the stock of my gun is the only thing which moves significantly as it slides up into the shoulder and cheek which are in a 'receive' position.

Having mounted the gun I track the target briefly before pulling through and pulling the trigger.

As the clay is broken I keep the stock in the cheek to maintain the smooth swing. I have shot the target in front for as it is a low driven bird if I leave it to come any closer it will present me with two problems: firstly, as it travels overhead it will demand a difficult physical manoeuvre,

Figure ii As the target comes towards me I keep the muzzles of the gun 'on' the clay as I mount the gun

Figure iii I track the target briefly

Figure iv As the clay is broken I keep the stock to my cheek

Figure v If there is a second clay flying at a moderate height, I will take it in front

With a low driven bird like the grouse it is best to take it in front, before it comes too close

and secondly, perhaps more importantly, by shooting it in front I give the shot pattern a chance to establish itself. If I were to leave the target until it was directly overhead then it would be similar to attempting to shoot it with a rifle. There would be no shot pattern, just a slender shot column. On the subject of pattern, an open bore is ideal for this kind of shot, either true cylinder or skeet. Similarly, size 9-shot cartridges.

I have also included an extra illustration in this sequence for sometimes this kind of bird is thrown in pairs. If they are low I would advocate attempting to shoot both in front, but if of moderate height then the second bird can be taken overhead. But think only of one target at a time, taking the straighter bird first. It will be the easier and can be dispatched more quickly with confidence. Then move on to the second one, going through the same procedure of tracking, moving through and shooting. Avoid the mistake of flashing at the second target. There is always more time than you think and many shots are missed by shooting too quickly and not really finding the line of the clay.

CROSSING PIGEON

Whereas with the driven grouse the shooter has to blot the target out with the muzzles of his gun as he shoots, with the crossing pigeon there is a requirement for definite forward allowance.

It has been calculated that a crossing woodpigeon at 30 yards would demand a forward allowance of 5 feet 6 inches, that is to say that the shooter would need to be aiming the gun at a point 5 feet 6 inches in front of the bird in order to hit it. At 40 yards this figure increases to 8 feet. I wouldn't suggest for a minute that you need to learn a set of tables so that you can work out the required forward allowance. I mention this to show what is required.

People can initially find it very difficult to shoot other than actually at a target. Thereafter, once they understand that a lead must be given, they often don't make it large enough. Nearly all crossing targets that are missed are missed behind, yet at any shooting school on any day of the year you will hear a pupil tell an instructor that he was in front of the target, he could not possibly have missed it behind. The same applies to high pheasant shooting. Virtually every shot is missed behind.

So why does it happen? The essential problem is that most people tend to be too stiff and mechanical when they are learning to shoot – indeed often they remain so throughout their entire shooting careers. They swing the gun in front of the clay, but stop to pull the trigger. It is barely discernible to them, so keen are they to hit the target, but they are lacking in confidence and want to make sure, whereas for good shooting you really have to be brave, pulling through the clay and squeezing the trigger at the optimum point without checking the gun's swing. Under the watchful eye of a good instructor this is soon detected and can be cured, but the pupil must place total faith in the instructor.

The instructor may also notice that the pupil is raising

his cheek slightly in order to see and double-check the whereabouts of the clay. This results in missing both behind and over the top. A raised cheek, no matter how slight, will alter the alignment of the barrel with the clay – half an inch at the stock can equate to a foot or more at 20 yards.

Keep it fluid and shoot with confidence. The rest will follow.

As you load the gun start the concentration process. Is your stance correct in relation to the target and where you take your shot? Do you know exactly where the target will come from and where you will be looking to shoot it?

Holding the gun in the direction of where the target will come into view, call 'PULL!' Note once again how the muzzles of the barrels are well up waiting on the flightline for the clay to appear.

As the clay comes towards the 'killing area' I have mounted on to it. Be careful of mounting too soon on a crossing target. If you sit on a target too long it tends to have a paralysing effect on your swing. Instead, track it smoothly and mount on to it by just sliding the stock into your shoulder and cheek.

Then move with it before swinging in front and squeezing the trigger. Keep those barrels moving smoothly throughout.

I often hear the question asked: 'How do I know how much forward allowance to give a crossing target at different distances?' Although many people jump in with their opinions, there is no given answer to this as it depends on the speed of swing of the shooter in question. Some very good shots say that they are totally unaware of any forward allowance – the fact is they probably swing their guns quite quickly and mount and shoot in one flowing motion. Their swing of the gun creates the forward allowance.

The brain is a wonderful computer and invariably the act of watching a target and tracking it will instinctively tell you how to respond. In any event if you have a good

Figure i As I load I start the concentration process – making sure I know where the clay will come from and checking my stance in relation to the target area

Figure ii Holding the gun in the direction from which the target will come into view, I call, 'PULL!'

Figure iii My head is well forward and, as the clay appears, I mount on to it

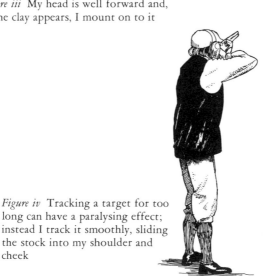

Figure iv Tracking a target for too long can have a paralysing effect; instead I track it smoothly, sliding the stock into my shoulder and cheek

Figure v I move with the clay – then swing in front and squeeze the trigger

instructor behind you, after three or four shots he will be able to understand your sight picture, your swing and what is needed.

The choke and cartridge combination depends on the range of the crosser but a ¼ choke and 8-shot cartridge are a sound combination for all but the extreme-range birds. You can then maybe step up to ½ choke.

As I call the crossing pigeon target I am poised and my barrels are well up

Having dealt with the incomer and crosser we now move to the going-away bird. Certainly, for novices without the assistance of an instructor, this is a much simpler shot than the crosser.

The going-away bird has much more in common with the instinct to rifle shoot than any other sporting target. Nevertheless, a number of mistakes can easily be made – there is no such thing as an easy clay on any round. They all have to be hit and the tendency is to relax on what are apparently simpler birds and consequently to drop two or three targets from a score which you know should have been better – the result sheet says maybe 37 out of 50, instead of 40.

It is noticeable also that many game shooters struggle on a relatively straightforward going-away bird. So why is this? Let's look at the sequence.

Note my footwork. I am standing with my body addressing the point at which I am going to shoot. The target will come from the trap house to my left and will quarter across me slightly. My stance encourages me to keep well forward and my head tight down on the stock for this target. The major worry is missing over the top. My belief is that many game shooters miss over the top of going-away targets simply because their gun is too light and they are not in control for the sort of precision shooting which is required.

The tendency is to rush through the target as it appears. The clay's trajectory is fairly flat, as it appears to climb but falls away quickly once it loses velocity. The game shot will swing through as though it is rising. The novice shooter will swing through and poke in panic. In fact there is usually plenty of time if you get yourself positioned properly and in a state of good mental preparation.

My head is well forward and as the target comes into view I mount on to it. As a trap shooter this is obviously a

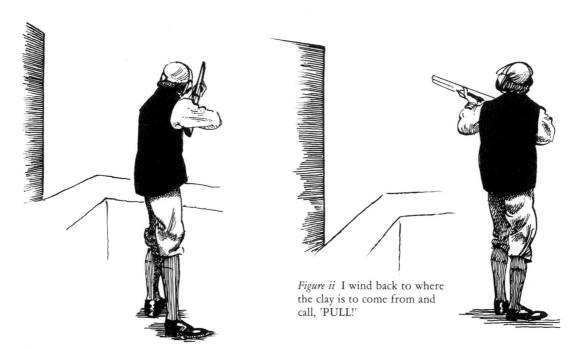

Figure i Note my footwork as I
calculate the point at which I will
shoot the target coming from my left

Figure ii I wind back to where
the clay is to come from and
call, 'PULL!'

I am well forward with my head
tight down on the stock – the major
worry is missing over the top

Figure iii My head is well
forward and as the target
comes into view I
mount on to it

Figure iv I must not wait too
long with a going-away bird
because it will become much
more difficult both with
distance and as a falling target

Figure v Having tracked briefly
to make sure of the line and
speed, I pull through slightly
because the target is quartering
across me, and I fire

target which comes easily to me. I have learned to lock into
going-away birds and to break them in one smooth flowing
motion. This is the easiest way to do it, for if you leave a
going-away target too long (probably to make sure) it will
become much more difficult both in distance and as it
becomes a dropping target.

So, having mounted on to the clay I track it briefly to
make sure of the line and the speed. Then I pull the trigger
to break the target. Note that because the target is quartering across me I have pulled through it slightly in order
to break it.

In a normal trap shooting situation my trap gun has ¾
full chokes, but seldom on a sporting layout do going away
birds need more than half choke. The ideal combination
is ¼/½.

RUNNING HARE

Running hare or bolting rabbit, it all amounts to much the same thing except that at Gleneagles the bolting rabbit is the right-to-left bird, while the running hare is the left-to-right. We have the layouts side-by-side. I have included the running hare in this chapter purely because we have already discussed right-to-left crossers, and this gives me an opportunity to look at the more difficult alternative.

Right-handed shooters find left-to-right crossers more difficult than the other way on. Similarly, left-handers prefer left-to-rights. There are a number of theories for this, the most common being that the right-hander naturally swings his arm across his body. To go away from the body is the equivalent of a backhand and consequently is a less natural movement. This makes a good deal of sense – that which you do naturally you do better. There is another argument that these birds represent an optical illusion for the right-handed shot because as the left-to-right is going across him his vision of the target is partially obscured by the gun moving through it. He consequently thinks he has given more forward allowance than he actually has.

Whatever the reason, in general terms it pays to give a little more lead to those targets which are crossing in the opposite direction to your natural hand.

The position of the body is absolutely crucial. You face the area at which you intend to take your shot then wind back to the source of the clay. The clay travels along the ground so you will need to make sure that you are standing in such a way that enables you to keep on top of the bird. Having stood facing the 'killing area', now turn back towards the trap house. Your muzzles will be held just high enough for you to be able to see the clay appear over the top of them. Now call the bird by saying, 'PULL!'

As the clay comes into view, you mount on to it. My feeling is that unlike other crossers you have relatively little time to shoot rabbits (or hares!) and it pays to pick up

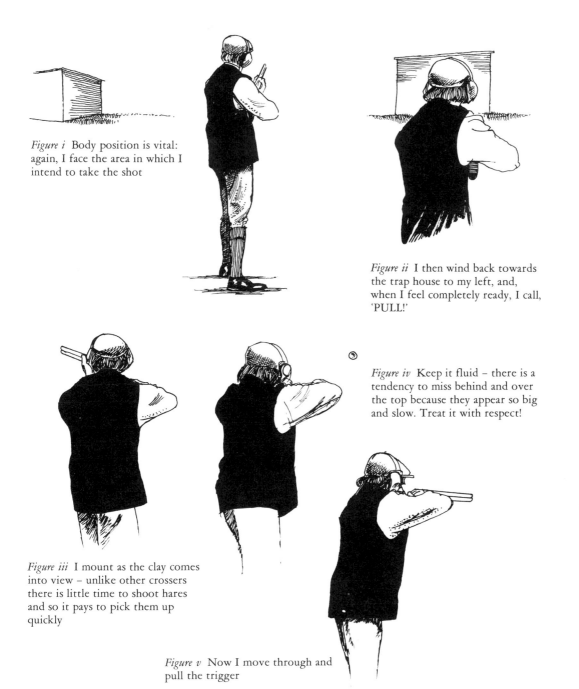

Figure i Body position is vital: again, I face the area in which I intend to take the shot

Figure ii I then wind back towards the trap house to my left, and, when I feel completely ready, I call, 'PULL!'

Figure iv Keep it fluid – there is a tendency to miss behind and over the top because they appear so big and slow. Treat it with respect!

Figure iii I mount as the clay comes into view – unlike other crossers there is little time to shoot hares and so it pays to pick them up quickly

Figure v Now I move through and pull the trigger

Running hare often appear to be so big and slow that you feel you cannot miss – but you do!

the line pretty quickly. Now move through and pull the trigger. The tendency with this type of clay is to shoot behind and over the top. They often appear to be so big and travelling so slowly that you feel you cannot miss – but you do, simply for not treating them with enough respect. Also because you are shooting downwards there is a tendency to peer over the barrels and lift your cheek off the stock. This will cause you to miss over the top and behind again.

Remember, keep it fluid and go for it.

The choke is not so important as the size of the shot. Always use 7-shot for rabbits – they are made to be quite tough so as not to break on impact with the ground. Small skeet pellets may fail to achieve the desired effect. Shoot trap cartridges and see them breaking into dust!

HIGH PHEASANT

The stand we call King's Tower at Gleneagles is, as mentioned earlier, a favourite of mine. Indeed this is the one which appeals most to all game shooters, simulating the ultimate sporting challenge, the high driven pheasant.

As you will notice from the photograph our tower has two automatic traps which move up and down the tower at the press of a button. This little piece of technology is a tremendous help enabling us to present a mix of targets at any height we choose.

As with the crossing bird mentioned earlier, most high pheasant shots are missed behind. Having tracked the bird and swung in front, you have to be brave enough to pull the trigger. It is perhaps instinctive to make sure by hesitating, but once you do this then the target is lost.

It is also advisable not to mount on to the bird too early. This is especially true for the real game shooting situation. If a driven pheasant appears in the sky some distance away there is always a temptation to mount on to it. 'Shoot in

With this device the traps on the high pheasant tower can be adjusted and so offer a mix of targets

front' are words of advice that echo from all sides. But this is only to be recommended for birds of modest height – any genuinely high birds should be allowed to come to the shooter thus presenting you with a better opportunity to assess speed and range.

You will notice how I am facing the direction from which the target is coming. As it comes into view my muzzles are raised so that I can track it over the tips of my barrels.

As it comes towards me I mount on to it to track the bird. Keeping a cool head is invaluable at this point. Take your time, for any bird that is hurried will be lost.

As the bird approaches between 10 and 11 o'clock swing through and shoot, remembering to pull the trigger on the swing.

Note that I have kept the weight on my front (left) foot. This not only looks more elegant but serves a very practical purpose in that it locks the head into the stock and prevents the stock from sliding off the shoulder. Some people shoot very well off the back foot but my feeling is that this method leaves the shooter prone to losing contact between cheek and stock. The shoulder can easily drop. Also in this illustration you will note that having taken the first shot and swung through I am immediately on to the second bird to be taken more or less overhead.

I must stress that an ability to keep cool and positive is a considerable advantage. Take a deep breath as you mount on to the target, keep the swing smooth and, in the instant that you feel the picture is right, pull the trigger. Don't hesitate for a second.

When it comes to choke and cartridge, though the birds are quite distant they are in full view of the muzzles and consequently will be well covered by the pattern. Some shooters prefer to use 9-shot cartridges on high driven clays in the knowledge that the weaker underside of the clay that is exposed to the shooter is easily broken. A fairly open choke is advisable too. Certainly ¼ choke and 8-shot

Figure i I face the direction of the trap with the barrels raised

Figure ii I mount on to the bird and track it

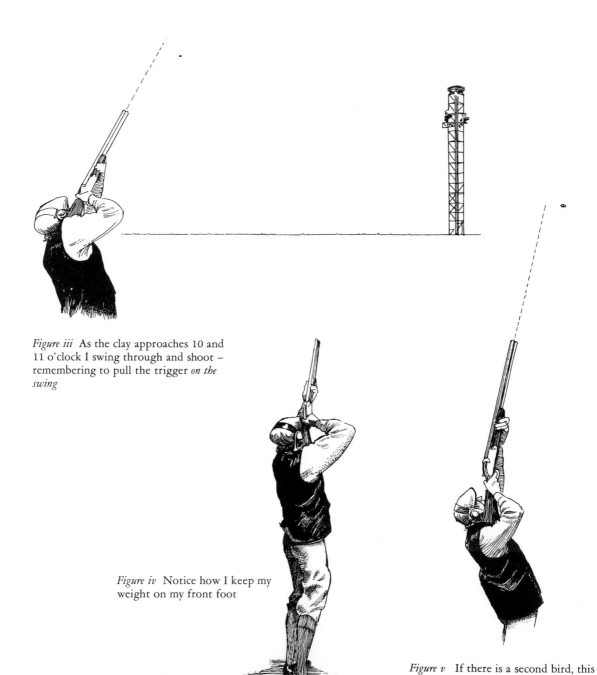

Figure iii As the clay approaches 10 and
11 o'clock I swing through and shoot –
remembering to pull the trigger *on the
swing*

Figure iv Notice how I keep my
weight on my front foot

Figure v If there is a second bird, this
is how I swing through to take it

cartridges are ample. In a game shooting situation I would use 7-shot to be sure of a clean kill.

For the extremely high birds that are presented on some of the more spectacular valley drives around the country, then there is a very good argument for using 6-shot where the extra penetration of bigger shot could be crucial.

The King's Tower at Gleneagles is a favourite of mine

The fur and feather stand is a good example of sporting on report targets. Using a combination of two very different targets the shooter is presented with a good, interesting test of his ability. His understanding of the principles of good shooting will be put to the test in his approach work, stance, and ability to mount and swing the gun properly.

For this particular sequence I have used the Gleneagles snipe and running hare stands. Each presents a different test to the shooter, the first being quite a precise shot and then turning for a smooth swing shot.

In a normal shooting situation you would probably watch others shoot before you took your turn. This should serve a useful purpose but be careful. It is easy to watch someone achieve a decent score on a stand while not realizing that they are shooting in a manner which you hadn't considered. Do not begin to attempt to copy them for you may miss four out of the first six targets before you realize that you have made a complete hash of the stand and by then it's too late. Other shooters will have styles completely different to your own, their speed and sight picture prompting them to respond in a certain way. Alternatively, you may watch an individual get a good score through shooting badly. He could simply have had a bit of luck but it won't stay with him all the way round the shoot. Seeing him could tempt you astray.

Instead you must concentrate on the targets rather than the person shooting them. Look for the points at which they appear and where you intend to take your shots. Above all else think in terms of 'one at a time'. In effect you are not shooting a pair but two singles.

When your name is called and it is your turn to shoot, your first priority is to make sure that you are standing in the correct position. Is it possible to shoot both targets from the same stance or do you need to move your feet between shots? This need not be a problem. Remember that the trapper cannot release the bird until he has heard your first shot. You are a jump ahead of him as only you know when you will pull the trigger. So with your gun still unloaded quickly rehearse your shots by facing the killing point of the second bird then turning back to the first. You will then know if you have to move. Double-check.

So, *Figure i* illustrates this, a quick rehearsal with an unloaded gun to see if the second bird can be shot without changing my stance. Now I will turn back to see if I can take the first bird from the same position. As it happens I

Figure i I quickly rehearse the shot with an unloaded gun to see if the second bird (a running hare) can be taken from the same position as the first (a snipe) – in this case it can

Figure ii I call the target – I'm quickly on to it

Figure iii I swing through and take it quickly before it loses momentum and falls

Figure iv On hearing my shot the trapper releases the running hare and I am soon tracking this second clay

can so I will now load my gun and collect my thoughts. Keep cool – one shot at a time.

The target has been called and I am quickly on to it. It is a relatively slow bird which enables me to pick it up quite soon after release.

Because of the target's slowness it is better to shoot it quickly in one flowing motion rather than to wait – it will become more difficult as it drops. As the clay loses its momentum so does the shooter.

I swing through the clay and break it cleanly. Having completed that shot I now transfer my attention to the running hare. The trapper has released the target on hearing my shot and I am in position ready once again to pick up the clay quite quickly.

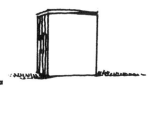

Figure v I complete the pair with my weight well
forward to avoid shooting over the top – always
a worry when shooting downwards

Having tracked the target I swing through and complete a successfully taken pair. Note how I have kept my weight well forward
to avoid the danger of shooting over the top of the target – always a
worry when you are shooting downwards.

Upon making my first
target I will swing through
for the running hare
already coming in from
the right

Other Sporting Targets

The possibilities in terms of sporting targets are endless. The three other principal types of bird to be considered are springing teal, 'overhead going-away' and simultaneous pairs.

The course organizer using the stands I have described plus these following three has plenty of variety at his disposal with which to entertain and challenge the shooter. The angles and speeds of the targets can, by slight variation, altogether alter the proposition. A quartering bird, such as a snipe or woodcock, if angled two yards further across the shooter than shown in the diagram, can become a very deceptive target. Similarly, if the crossing target loses its speed while crossing in front of the shooting position, it looks easy but is in fact more difficult!

Let us look at the other three principal sporting stations:

SPRINGING TEAL

Named after the teal which springs off the water almost vertically into the air, the springing teal stand involves a target (or pair of targets) which are angled upwards at around 70°. The trap will be in front of the shooter, and throw the clay directly up and away.

It rises quickly into the air and it should be remembered that it is at maximum speed on leaving the trap. If you pre-mount your gun you will most likely find that you will lose control of it as you chase the clay. Better to hold the gun out of the shoulder with the muzzles about one-third of the way up the clay's flight line. Call the bird and watch it emerge, then mount on to it, track it briefly and swing through and shoot as it reaches towards the top of its climb.

Some people prefer to wait until it reaches the top, but this can become a test of nerve and if you don't get it exactly right the target is easily missed over the top at this point. It looks to be stationary for a second but I have never yet come across an airborne clay pigeon which isn't moving!

You will also find that if the stand involves a pair of targets together from the teal trap, by shooting the first clay whilst travelling upwards, there is still time to hit the other one before it gets to the top.

Watch also for an angle. If the clay is veering right or left, make sure that your swing follows the projected line. Don't just swing and hope.

OVERHEAD GOING-AWAY

Often known as 'overhead pigeon' or 'landing duck', these are targets which are generally thrown from a low tower to the rear of the shooting position.

The main point to remember is that as the target flies over your head and away from you, it is at all times dropping. As I said earlier, don't lift your head to look at the clay – this is the stand where such a movement is all too easy. Keep the cheek locked into your stock.

Let's go back to the beginning. On this target you will stand as normal, facing the area at which you intend to shoot. Then looking directly upwards so that you can see the clay come into view, you ease your body weight back on to your right leg. You will hold your gun so that your muzzles are almost vertical.

When you are ready, you call, 'PULL!' As the clay comes into view, mount on to it transferring your weight on to your left leg as it passes overhead. Then, after briefly tracking the clay, push through it and pull the trigger. Keep it smooth and fluid. The head-lifting problem occurs when a pair of targets is thrown. After the first shot, it is tempting to lift the head to find the second clay. Don't do it – keeping your head on the stock, find the target and shoot just underneath it. Knock its boots off!

PAIRS

Watching people shoot pairs of clays I often notice inconsistencies creep into their performance. They may shoot the first of a pair and miss the second, then the next time miss the first and hit the second. Clearly, they know how to break both clays, so why don't they hit the pair?

Mostly this is down to approach work. Before taking the shots it is vital to be absolutely clear in your own mind exactly how you intend to take them. With clay pigeon shooting you will always know exactly where the clays are coming from and where they are going to. So, if the targets are crossing from left to right, you firstly have to decide which target to shoot first and where to take it.

How do you decide? With crossers the answer is simple. You always take the back one first, which then enables you to naturally swing on to the front one. Your next decision will be to decide where the second shot will be taken. You then prepare yourself for the shot by positioning yourself for the second shot, and winding yourself back to take the first. Then you call the clay. There may even be enough time between shots to move your feet.

The most common fault is that people find they are in a good position for the first one, but then are straining to get on to the second. It always has to be one shot at a time. Be methodical and keep it simple. There is always so much more time than you think.

On driven or going-away pairs, I find that it is best to take the straighter bird first. There are two reasons for this: firstly, it is the simplest shot and so can be quickly dealt with, and secondly, after shooting the first target you will swing naturally in the direction of the angled target. Conversely, if you shoot the angled target first, picking up the line of a straight target calls for mid-swing readjustment. And you don't want to make life complicated for yourself!

Finally, the other point to remember about pairs is . . .

keep your head down! Yes, I know that I am labouring the point but it really is important. Don't whatever you do lift your head after the first shot – once you have pulled the trigger, just keep in total control of the gun and think in terms of nothing else but picking up the line of the second clay. Hit or missed, the first target is history.

Targets

The sporting course organizer also has a number of targets at his disposal, so always make sure you know what kind of clay you are shooting at. What might appear to be a very long-range clay may well be a midi. You might have fed your personal computer (the brain!) with the wrong information and instead of prompting the necessary forward allowance to break a midi at 25 yards it will have been deceived into thinking in terms of a standard at 40 yards. A miss will result.

Other points to remember are that rabbit targets are made of a tougher composition so that they don't break on impact with the ground. You should therefore resist the temptation of using 9-shot cartridges – the small pellets may lack sufficient impact to break the target.

Battues are amusing targets. They have no lip so consequently they tend to twist and turn in flight. A thrown battue may come into view 'flat on' to the shooter, looking like a huge unmissable black saucer. But by the time it reaches the shooting position it may have twisted edge-on offering only a thin line to aim at. Again you will need 7-shot and a tighter-choked barrel to make sure of a kill.

And remember to wear a pair of glasses if you are shooting a driven bird of any sort. You wouldn't want a chip of clay in your eye – and you may find that the lenses help your visibility, particularly on a bright sunny day.

A selection of clay pigeons – the brighter coloured ones are the same as the black but are for use against a dark background

> *Top pair:* Rabbit clays – note the reinforced lip to avoid breakage on contact
>   with the ground
> *Outside pair:* Standard (110mm diameter)
> *Inside pair:* Midi (90mm)
> *Second from bottom:* Battue – this has no lip and so it twists in the air
> *Bottom pair:* Mini (60 mm) – this clay is only used occasionally

FITASC Sporting

The origins of FITASC sporting are somewhat obscure. Its name is an abbreviation of its ruling body, Fédération Internationale de Tir aux Armes Sportives de Chasse, which is based in Paris. France is widely regarded as the home of FITASC sporting. Although most of the major competitions are won by British shooters, France has a monopoly of the quality venues and most years they play host to either the World or European championships.

FITASC should more properly be called International Sporting, as this is the form in which the discipline is recognized in many countries around the world. All World and European championships are shot to FITASC rules.

So how does FITASC differ from regular 'English' sporting? Principally, it is very much more sophisticated. From the outset the concept of our sporting has always been to simulate the flight of quarry species (springing teal, crossing pigeon, and so on), but at any sporting shoot the competitor is asked to shoot five identical pairs of targets. When did you last see ten quail cross in front on exactly the same flightline at exactly the same speed? The underlying principle of FITASC, therefore, is that no two targets are alike, and every shot is a new and fresh challenge. As such it is considered by many to be the ultimate simulation of game shooting (hunting). In fact it is invariably very much more difficult than real game is ever likely to be.

Yet, despite this it is a discipline which can be enjoyed by the average sporting shooter. There are some targets that he will find very difficult, but there are others that are very simple. Its appeal lies in the sheer variety of quality targets and as such it is a true test of shooting ability embracing the many facets involved, including gun handling, positioning, and the mental agility to read the targets and sustain concentration under pressure.

With few exceptions, prize money has never figured

strongly in FITASC. Experienced shooters regard FITASC as the cream and participate purely for the challenge. Also every shooter of note would love to get his hands on the World Championship trophy! There are many titles, some very important, but in golf there is only one British Open, in tennis only one Wimbledon and in sporting clay shooting only one World Championship.

Let us look at how FITASC competitions are orchestrated. Any experienced course designer will relish the challenge of putting together a FITASC layout every bit as much as the shooter will enjoy coming to terms with it. With a combination of ingenuity and common sense, the good course organizer will create the kind of challenge which makes FITASC so special.

Most of the major shoots are held over 150 or 200 targets, but it is perfectly possible to stage any kind of FITASC shoot in permutations of 25 birds. A 100-bird competition, for example, will be held on four 25-bird layouts. Each of these layouts will have three or four different shooting positions and utilize up to six traps (or a minimum of three). If you look at the diagram you will note how by simply moving the shooting position, the nature of a target can be altered dramatically. From Station Two on the diagram, for instance, the target from Trap B (installed in a tower) is a simple driven bird – but from Station Three this becomes a high right-to-left crosser.

A mixture of target sizes will also be used, along with angles, elevations, speeds, towers and so on.

All of the shooting is undertaken in squads of six guns. On a four-stand layout, three singles and two doubles will be shot on the first stand, with full use of gun (i.e. both barrels) on all singles. This, I feel, is a small but significant aspect of FITASC, because some of the very best shots are often taken second barrel. The gun must be well out of the shoulder (below shoulder level) when the target is called. Pre-mounting is not allowed.

The singles are shot by each member of the squad before

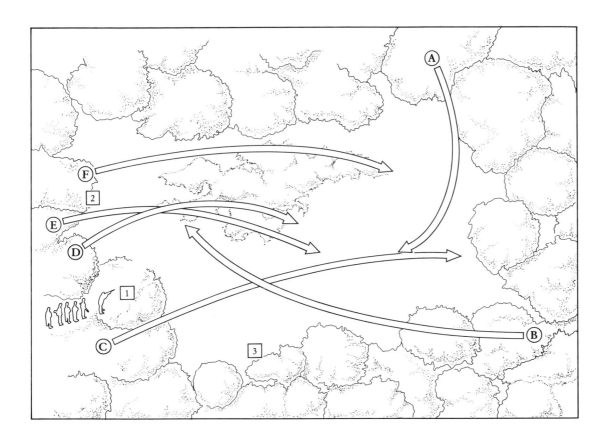

FITASC sporting layout: In groups of six, the shooters take turns at each station. A typical layout might have the following pattern of targets:

STAND	FORM	TRAP	TYPE OF CLAY	STAND	FORM	TRAP	TYPE OF CLAY
1	Singles	A	Standard	3	Singles	A	Standard
		B	Standard			B	Standard
		C	Midi			D	Rabbit
		D	Rabbit			E	Midi
		E	Midi		Doubles	A+E	Standard+Midi
	Doubles	C+B	Midi+Standard			B+D	Standard+Rabbit
		A+D	Standard+Rabbit				
2	Singles	A	Standard				
		B	Standard				
		E	Midi				
		F	Standard White				
	Doubles	A+A	Midi+Standard				

the second member of the squad starts with the doubles. The squad then moves on to Station Two where there are two singles and two doubles, the third person in the squad being the first to shoot the singles. The fourth kicks off the doubles.

Station Three will again offer two singles and two doubles, with the fifth and sixth members of the squad being first and second to shoot, respectively. Finally, to Station Four for two singles and two doubles to complete the 25 targets.

The sequence of 25 birds takes approximately 45 to 50 minutes. It is a period of time during which the shooter will savour a whole range of emotions – the highs of hitting a difficult target, the lows of missing a simple one, handling the pressure when the misses come thick and fast and keeping it together when the adrenaline starts to flow. Most shooters find that they are competing with no one other than themselves when on a FITASC layout. Concentration must be sustained and many find that maximum results are achieved by switching off and on, as and when needed.

There is also a certain camaraderie which is built up between the six shooters, who will stay together through the duration of the competion. It is common for shooters to help one another, identifying strengths and weaknesses and sharing those highs and lows.

So why, you may ask, is FITASC not more popular? Certainly, it carries a growing but still relatively small following in the UK. Even in mainland Europe where FITASC is the dominant discipline, sporting is yet to realize its full potential.

So, to begin with, newcomers to shooting would find FITASC too difficult. It is not a discipline for the novice, therefore it doesn't attract people to the sport. People who take up shooting want the satisfaction of breaking clays and there are nursery slopes in clay shooting just like in skiing or the equivalent in other sports. Also, compared to

FITASC sporting is more sophisticated than 'English', providing a more authentic simulation of the game shooting situation

English sporting, FITASC is expensive. It takes more traps, more trappers, more land and more office staff and yet can handle relatively few entries. A 150-bird shoot held over two days using six different layouts can take a maximum of 144 people. The going rate for entry fees is around £70 with very modest prize-money. A two-day shoot will also inevitably involve hotel bills. So it's not a loose-change sport. Also of course there is the time factor to be considered. And from an organizer's point of view, staging such an event can cause logistical problems.

The rules, however, have now been relaxed to accommodate more entries and this may prove beneficial to the sport in two ways: it becomes more financially viable for the organizer and it permits more people to take part and consequently helps the sport grow. Whereas before only one squad of six shooters would be allowed on to a 25-bird layout, the sequence of 25 can now be arranged so that three squads shoot at the same time.

The 1990 World Championship at Le Rabot, France, ran to the new system and was voted a great success by all of the 700-plus competitors (especially by Britain's Michael Rouse who won the event in a remarkable year which also saw him win the World Cup Series and the European Championship).

Afterword

I hope that this book has been instructive for those coming fresh to clay shooting, and that it has been useful and entertaining to more experienced shots. As you have seen, this is a relatively old sport with etiquette and time-honoured traditions deeply ingrained into the heart of a day's shooting. And I believe that it has a great future too – with the prestige and glamour which have remained associated with the sport attracting large numbers of people, and with new developments always adding to the competitive challenge and safety.

Guns and ammunition have come a long way over the years, but there are still improvements to be made. Environmentally there can be many improvements, such as cartridges with quieter detonations and with both casings and shot which are kinder to the Earth. There is also room for plenty more investment in the development of shotgun design. The gun still has various unpleasant side-effects in terms of noise and recoil, and some designs are inflexible for use across a range of disciplines. There will always be a place, however, for the 'English gun', a classic design the financial and aesthetic values of which are forever escalating whether for the collector or the user.

I am sure that shooting facilities and clubs like the one we have developed at Gleneagles will become increasingly common. In such comfortable and friendly surroundings as these I forsee ever-greater numbers of men and women, young and old, coming into the sport. At all levels, the sport can be made still more enjoyable with such investment. Not only will the tremendous challenge of shooting be available to an ever-increasing number of people, but also the wider range of facilities and shooting disciplines will make the experience that much more rewarding. As with all sports, greater competition and interest at a grass-roots level inevitably has a beneficial effect on standards of competition at the top, and this is a phenomenon we have already experienced in shooting in Britain.

The best example of this is women's shooting. Over the past few years we have already seen a marked increase in the number of women entering the sport, many of them showing a remarkable natural instinct with a gun, and these women have developed their talents extremely impresssively. As a result, women's categories in the open championships have become highly competitive and participants are experiencing ever-higher demands on their skills and greater satisfaction as a result.

Shooting has been of tremendous value to me in my life in a variety of ways. It helped me develop as a person and through shooting I have got to know some wonderful people whom I would otherwise never have met. This is the shooting fraternity which I would urge anyone to aspire to.

Whether you are a beginner or an experienced shot, I hope that reading this book has not only given you an insight into the technical aspects of clay shooting, but that it has also put across some of the passion I feel for the sport and the enjoyment I have had through my dedication to every aspect of learning and improving my clay shooting. If you should experience even a fraction of the pleasure I have had in this sport then that will be a very great pleasure indeed.

Good luck and happy shooting!

Index